RHETORIC, POWER AND COMMUNITY

Rhetoric, Power and Community

An exercise in reserve

David Jasper

Director of the Centre for the
Study of Literature and Theology
University of Glasgow

Westminster / John Knox Press
Louisville, Kentucky

First published in Great Britain in 1993
by The Macmillan Press Ltd

First American edition

Published by Westminster / John Knox Press
Louisville, Kentucky

Printed in Hong Kong

9 8 7 6 5 4 3 2 1

Library of Congress Cataloging-in-Publication Data
Jasper, David
    Rhetoric, power and community : an exercise in reserve / David
Jasper.
        p.   cm.
    Includes bibliographical references and index.
    ISBN 0–884–25434–9 (pbk.)
        1. Rhetoric—Religious aspects—Christianity.   2. Rhetoric in the
Bible,   3. Bible.   N. T. —Criticism, interpretation, etc.
4. Christianity and literature.   I. Title.
BR115.R55J37   1993
808'.06623—dc20   92–18357

For Liz

Contents

Preface

I cannot promise that this book will provide easy reading. It is, to say the least, provisional, a series of explorations which, quite deliberately, do not constitute an argument but together try to feel their way out of one situation and towards the possibility of another. Partly, also, I am engaged in a very personal exercise to do with faith, theology, and the instruments of religious discourse which I have inherited from within the Christian Church, from academic study and the experience of liturgy, and from an inescapable fascination with the dialogue of modern and post-modern literary criticism and theory. I am at once bound and liberated as well by a love of literature which is for me an addiction and a necessity. My anxieties and preoccupations turn, and turn again, within the text, and if there is an indecency in that, I am not, at this stage, going to apologise. A reader, after all, must exercise the freedom to accept or reject what is set before him.

I am concerned with rhetoric, and in particular the rhetoric of religious texts of various kinds, insofar as it is involved with persuasion and the exercise of power, and trying to identify where power resides in the processes of textuality. Specific texts in scripture, liturgy, theology and literature will be studied upon the model of a community (the church) in search of identity by means of 'contextualisation' – engaging in self-reflective activity in the formation of a text whereby power is wielded and the community enforced.

The question must then be asked, what role is theology playing in these processes, and where, in such rhetorical manipulations, is God to be found? Beginning with Plato's suspicion and Aristotle's defence of rhetoric, I will go on to examine the 'radical' Christian rhetoric of the New Testament, and in particular St Mark's Gospel and the letters of St Paul, and their relationship with classical rhetoric as a language of persuasion and power.

If the historian Eusebius is to be believed, St Mark's Gospel arose out of the departure of St Peter from the local church and the need felt as a result to establish a text by which the community could define and preserve its origins and nature. The Pauline epistles also provide a textual authority for the churches in the absence of the apostle himself. Various models of community need to be examined. St Mark's Gospel could be read as the text of a community which has been formed upon the threat of individual alienation, a threat imposed by the rhetoric of the Gospel. Or does a closer examination in terms of classical rhetorical tropes – and particularly irony – reveal a community much closer in nature to the Pauline image of the Body of Christ?

The recognition of Jesus as Messiah requires an acknowledgement of a profound discontinuity in the tradition of the 'Book' – which tradition Jesus both fulfils and radically disturbs. The Reformation era is similarly a moment of discontinuity in the tradition of the Western Church and its self-understanding in text. Chapter 5 is a close reading of the rhetoric of the Holy Communion service of Cranmer's prayer book of 1549 (a thoroughly Lutheran document), arguing that its 'rhetoric of discontinuity' establishes a powerful cohesive force, much as St Mark's Gospel does, in a community which is intensely aware of both its sinfulness and its authority. Here rhetoric and doctrinal understanding are inextricably linked.

The later chapters of the book move more specifically into the modern and postmodern world. Texts like Mikhail Bakhtin's great study of Rabelais, deeply revolutionary, deeply religious and written under terrible political pressure, emerge from a century which, after Nietzsche, has experienced both the collapse of metaphysics and a vivid, deconstructive sense of loss in certainties in the traditional claims of religion and its language. Discontinuity has, at last, become not only a moment of power in the politics of our time, but has also surfaced in unbearable neuroses and the loss of individual and communal consciousness. But does this very loss, ironically, strike a note of hope?

Theology has always been obsessed with power and authority – the authority, perhaps, of God, or the Church, or individuals within the church. Through rhetoric and rhetorical criticism we come to see how the Western tradition has defined itself in text, has been defined by text, and reconstitutes itself through repeated experiences of discontinuity, through an entextualising process which both forms community and perhaps suggests the nature and purpose of the religious community. Or might it be that through a further rhetorical exercise, and ironically, the expectations of theology must be finally deconstructed and hope unfettered in a new and unexpected linguistic freedom?

It might well be suggested that my perspective is peculiarly English, not to say Anglican. That is hardly surprising, though a book which embraces on its first page the Prague Spring, Michel Foucault, Bakhtin, Rabelais and Nietzsche is barely to be called parochial in its reference. But I have deliberately chosen as my text examples from scripture, from the liturgy, and from literature, taken as broadly as possible. Not everyone, of course, will respond to my particular sense of the Book of Common Prayer. But there will no doubt be other texts which would do just as well from other traditions, and what is important is the argument, with its sense of power and violence operating through textual means. If other texts do better for you, try them (as Coleridge would have said) and see.

In this book I do not claim to be systematic or to offer a comprehensive reader's guide to rhetorical criticism or the study of rhetoric. I have been, sometimes deliberately, cavalier in my interpretations, and I leave the reader to decide if I am playing a game or simply being perverse. No doubt sometimes I am plain wrong and I am content to be told so. These explorations are an attempt to clear ground and I would expect a further stage to be explored in another book as yet unwritten. I am indebted to very many people and not least the long-suffering postgraduate students of Durham university upon whom I have tried out ideas. Three colleagues in Durham, Ann Loades, Richard Roberts and Peter Malekin, patiently read numerous drafts as chapters took shape. I would like to thank also Robert Detweiler, Mark Ledbetter, Stephen Prickett, Linda Munk, Tibor Fabiny, Kirsten Nielsen, Dennis Stamps, Stephen Finley, Brayton Polka and Werner Jeanrond who have helped me more than they may be aware. Frances Arnold, my publisher, has seen the project to completion with exemplary courtesy and professionalism. Mrs Andrea Marshall typed my manuscript into a readable form. My wife Alison and our three daughters have borne with my preoccupations with cheerful stoicism, Hannah, the eldest, being a natural deconstructer and ironist.

An earlier version of Chapter 4 was published in *The Bible as Rhetoric, Studies in Biblical Persuasion and Credibility*, edited by Martin Warner and published by Routledge (1990). An earlier version of Chapter 7 is to be published by Bristol Press (1991) in *The Recovery of Rhetoric: Persuasive Discourse and Interdisciplinarity in the Human Sciences*, edited by Richard H. Roberts and J.M.M. Good. I am very grateful for permissions granted to use this material again in a revised form.

The publishers and author gratefully acknowledge the permission granted to reproduce, in full, D.J. Enright, 'History of World Languages', from *Collected Poems* (1987, Oxford University Press, licensing agents Watson, Little Limited).

David Jasper, Glasgow

1

Introduction: Nietzschean Hilarity

> I was stunned by the realisation that this was possible: that she could yearn for me and make love to another and weep for another, yet life was like that, that things panned out like that.
>
> Ivan Klima[1]

In Ivan Klima's fictional world, dominated by the experience of the Prague Spring when he was editor of the journal of the Czech Writers' Union, it is impossible to find out the truth about anything. It is a world of betrayal and disillusionment in which truth is forsaken for power of a particular, coercive kind, and such power is detached from the power of truth which is complex, elusive and often seemingly contradictory.[2]

The status of truth, in Foucault's phrase, will be the underlying theme of this study. My ambition, therefore, is considerable, and it may be felt that my achievement is meagre. But as an exercise in rhetoric which is deeply suspicious of rhetoric, and therefore suspicious of itself, the book claims only to be a beginning, and to sound warnings and establish some possible directions for future, necessarily constructive theological reflections. Chapter 6 gives some attention to Mikhail Bakhtin's great study of François Rabelais, the inventor of the now-forgotten neologism, *agelaste*, which means a man who does not laugh and who has no sense of humour.[3] Rabelais feared such a man. For the *agelaste* is convinced that the truth is simple and obvious and that its certainty not only may but should be imposed upon all. Against this seriousness the novelist Milan Kundera sets the laughter of God, for such divine laughter perceives not only the danger but the self-defeating processes of the *agelaste*'s thought: the more he thinks monologically, the more his thought diverges from the thought of others, the more isolated his 'truth'. The alternative is to listen to God's laughter in its wisdom and complexity, God's rhetoric a deconstructive rhetoric, even, perhaps a Nietzschean hilarity. In what follows, I will try to explain, if only by indirection – as an attempt to escape by rhetoric the rhetorical circle – what I mean by this odd suggestion.

Losing the certainty of truth, one dares to become an individual. My intention is not to offer a history of rhetoric, or even to offer a guide to rhetorical practice and the numerous studies now available of it. Others have done that already and the bibliography at the end of this book will introduce the reader to the field.[4] I intend, rather, to pursue, by means of my own particular rhetoric, since rhetoric cannot be eschewed, a religious preoccupation with the power of the art of linguistic persuasion as it is exercised upon the community which is bound together by common religious beliefs. I am led to ask the questions, in what sense is the truth claimed by such an exclusive community true, and what is the relationship between truth and power? The status and importance of texts in the Western tradition of such communities is unavoidable, whether those texts be scriptual, liturgical or theological, and as rhetoric is obsessed with persuasion and power, I am concerned to track down in the dynamism of the reading process and in the convergence of text and reader the creative point at which the communal effect of a text is enforced and the community of readers both discovers itself and maintains its identity.

The final questions remain. What is the place of traditional Christian theology in this game, and where is the God of our tradition in it?

A problem for a study of rhetoric is that one can never stand outside rhetoric. It is, by its very nature, itself rhetorical.[5] The problem is examined in some detail in Chapter 7 in a discussion of Freud and Stanley Fish. A theory of rhetoric entails an act of exclusive idealisation which, like most theology for the believing community, wraps linguistic activity around and guarantees a sense of meaningfulness within the security of its universal, artificial claims of system. But what are the consequences if the business is studied from within, without the benefit of exclusive claims or master roles? Is it possible to 'do theology' in such a deconstructive, Derridian way, refusing to be comforted by the assurance that there is a safe and consoling point of reference providing a privileged point of access to the text,[6] any readily identifiable authorial intentionality or metaphysical security? Refusing such neutral rationality – wielding as it does the coercive force of Dostoyevsky's Grand Inquisitor – one opts instead for a more dangerous and complex freedom within the inconclusive, shrewd, ironic, oblique possibilities of verbal and textual interplay. The point is not to uncover rhetoric in order to reach the Truth. Rather one must engage with rhetorical practice and play with its cunning in order, perhaps, to celebrate one's freedom from its tendency to make large claims to suit its own ends.

At best one celebrates the departure of the demands of wisdom, in an endless celebration of truth which is perceived by Paul de Man in Nietzschean terms as 'a moving army of metaphors, metonymies and anthropomorphisms',[7] itself rhetorical and an innoculation against the corrosive effects of textual closure, even the closure implied in the conclusion that there is no closure. In de Man's words, 'A text like [Nietzsche's] *On Truth and Lie*, although it presents itself legitimately as a demystification of literary rhetoric remains entirely literary, rhetorical, and deceptive itself'.[8]

One has to remain ever conscious of the irony of the insight. It is all too easy to become deceitful through the sense of one's own deconstructive practice, the worst and most cynical kind of self-assertion. Drawing on his reading of Nietzsche, de Man moves beyond his sense of the disruption between the grammatical and the rhetorical (or performative) in discourse, to the very questioning of the possibility of performativity.[9]

Performance being itself linguistic, and therefore rhetorical, irreducibly tropological, how can we actually know whether we are doing anything or not? The discourse both proposes and rhetorically disposes of itself. This collapse of meaning lies at the heart of the experience of the prophet Jonah. As Terry Eagleton describes Jonah's unwilling missionary journey to Nineveh, ' . . . even if he could console himself by surmising that his journey really was necessary, that this crying doom was performatively effective rather than farcically redundant, there is no way in which he can ever know this for certain, no way in which he can ever know whether he was doing anything or not![10] How far is Jonah an agent of God, or merely a participant in the divine narrative, a privileged actor denouncing a sinful city, or a tool in a greater game who can at best respond with petulant, ineffective anger (Jonah 4:9)? Jonah may think, like most people in his position, that he occupies a meta-position outside the narrative, and is understanding if not indeed controlling God himself, but he is, in fact, supremely controlled within the text itself. Eagleton concludes that 'Jonah just has to find some way of living with the fact that he can never know whether he is doing anything or not, which was perhaps the point of the whole futile narrative after all.'[11]

Who can ever know what it is to know nothing? Far from being meaningless, that may be the most meaningful of questions, a recognition, as Jonah recognises, of the necessary, perpetual displacement of false security and assumption in the experience of textuality: that our

establishment of an apparatus of power, in religious doctrine or ecclesiastical institution, will always be undercut
by a greater freedom and by the infinite complexity of the
rhetoric of the text.

I would wish to transfer the apparatus of power as it is
applied by Michel Foucault to the state, to the church or
religious community. As Foucault puts it:

> To pose the problem in terms of the State means to
> continue posing it in terms of sovereign and sover-
> eignty, that is to say in terms of law. If one describes all
> these phenomena of power as dependant on the state
> apparatus, this means grasping them as essentially
> repressive: the Army as a power of death, police and
> justice as punitive instances, etc. I don't want to say
> that the State isn't important; what I want to say is that
> relations of power, and hence the analysis that must be
> made of them, necessarily extend beyond the limits of
> the State. In two senses: first of all because the State, for
> all the omnipotence of its apparatuses, is far from be-
> ing able to occupy the whole field of actual power
> relations, and further because the State can only operate
> on the basis of other, already existing power relations.
> The State is superstructural in relation to a whole series
> of power networks that invest the body, sexuality, the
> family, kinship, knowledge, technology and so forth.[12]

Under the state we are under law, but in these circumstances what of grace? In church, as in state, a rhetoric of
power may effectively impose order and demand commitment by threat or promise. But within this context,
how may one release into a new freedom those deeper,
more elusive relations of power upon which the state
rhetoric plays its games and which (perhaps like Jonah's
God) it exploits for its own survival? Christian theology
has enjoyed dictating attitudes towards sexuality, the
family, kinship, knowledge and even technology (science
has often suffered at the hands of various kinds of

repressive fundamentalism), but rarely has it allowed them the freedom of their natures. Their own rhetorical play of textuality in literature and art has too often been suppressed and condemned as naught(y) – against the rules – with the resultant neurosis all too frequently apparent in church communities.

Modern theology, like the politics of our century, has signally failed to take Nietzsche, and all that has followed in his admonitory wake, seriously enough. I want to take his last two books, written just before insanity finally overtook him, both immensely seriously and yet idiosyncratically so. As with my reading of Plato's *Phaedrus* in Chapter 2, I am not concerned so much with a 'right' critical reading, but with what Harold Bloom might call a 'strong' reading, a reading which provokes and empowers the reader to disagree, to think for herself, to realise herself at the cost of the author. The ironist is never fully to be trusted, his influence productive of an anxiety which may thankfully represent a freedom from the communal enthralment to text. One can but say with Coleridge that one is dealing not with Theory or Speculation, but a Life and a living Process: TRY IT.[13]

In *Twilight of the Idols* (1889) and *The Anti-Christ* (1895), Nietzsche makes an assault on institutional Christianity, presenting us with the 'Dionysian' artist and his only worthy opponent, Christ himself. In the early chapters of *Twilight of the Idols*, Socrates figures largely as 'the buffoon who *got himself taken seriously*'[14] – a *decadent* or an *agelaste*? Socrates, the ironist, was fascinating, representing for Nietzsche, with the whole Christian tradition, a 'misunderstanding' as a 'morality of improvement':

> The harshest daylight, rationality at any cost, life bright, cold, circumspect, conscious, without instinct, in opposition to the instincts, has itself been no more than a form of sickness, another form of sickness – and by no means a way back to 'virtue', to 'health', to happiness . . .[15]

But was Socrates merely a shrewd 'self-deceiver'? Is not the imitation of Socratic reasoning, paradoxically, the sacrifice of reason by reason: as rhetoric deconstructs itself? Socrates will speak for himself in the *Phaedrus* in Chapter 2, intertwined with a rhetorical context of intertextuality which continually outflanks its own devices.

The deconstructive, postmodern world is not a slave to formalism. Indeed, quite the contrary. For, in Jean-François Lyotard's definition, 'the postmodern would be that which, in the modern, puts forward the unpresentable in presentation itself; that which denies itself the solace of good forms, the consensus of a taste which would make it possible to share collectively the nostalgia for the unattainable: that which searches for new presentations, not in order to enjoy them but in order to impart a stronger sense of the unpresentable'.[16] The post-modern, deconstructed world is not, then, without consensus and community. But its community is not by nature the community which is bound by the architectural, rhetorical principles defined in *Twilight of the Idols*:

> The most powerful men have always inspired the architects: the architect has always been influenced by power. Pride, victory over weight and gravity, the will to power, seek to render themselves visible in a building; architecture is a kind of rhetoric of power, now persuasive, even cajoling in form, now bluntly imperious.[17]

Such powerful, coercive architectural rhetoric is, of course, deeply embedded in New Testament imagery, in St Matthew's 'stone which the builders rejected' (21: 42, drawing upon Psalm 118: 22[18]) and the 'choice corner-stone of great worth' of I Peter 2: 6 (from Isaiah 28: 16), and its formalist coercion is epitomised for Nietzsche in the rhetoric of St Paul whose writings are deliberately subjected to Nietzschean scrutiny in Chapter 3 of this study. In Nietzsche's words in *The Anti-Christ*:

> . . . Paul willed the end, *consequently* he willed the means . . . What he himself did not believe was believed by the idiots among whom he cast *his* teaching – *His* requirement was *power*; with Paul the priest again sought power – he could employ only those concepts, teachings, symbols with which one tyrannises over masses, forms herds.[19]

How far this must be read in the context of my own subsequent discussion, the reader must decide for himself. 'Let the reader understand' (Mark 13: 14) sounds the note of warning that the abomination of desolation may be 'the already irresistible corruption *within* the first community',[20] evidenced in their very sacred texts, yet the warning note may also indicate a way out, in literary terms, by the ironic textual interplay between surface and deep structure.

But what lies beneath this revealing textual decay? A close, deconstructive re-reading of the key terms of sacred scripture will lead us to disintegrate the convoluted theology with which the church has protected the person of Jesus 'almost like a way of protecting itself from the explosive implications of what were probably his most genuine teachings'.[21] Jesus' inherent failure is rarely taken seriously enough in the history of Christian triumphalism with its craving for salvation at any cost, its dialogue with a particular kind of power which renders its communities quiescent, and an unwillingness (for moral reasons) to take seriously the Dionysian element in the Judaeo-Christian context.[22] The dismal failure of Christian attempts to address the problem of theodicy stems largely from its moral timidity and fear of recognising that the battle between Christ and the Devil emerges from a bifurcation of the ancient, Dionysian male deity of the old religion of the agrarian underclasses.[23] Thus one critic, not unreasonably, concludes:

> Christians finally cut themselves off from nature-oriented sensibilities and relegated sex and women to an inferior status. The religious experience itself – so elusive of control and definition and even wild and subversive in the Dionysian tradition – was now safely channelled and controlled through the sacraments of a hierarchical, authoritarian, male-dominated Church.[24]

The chapters of this book risk an anger with the self-satisfaction of this Christian control, a rhetorical anger which speaks against itself in excess, and is necessary, dangerous, properly containing its own death. As Roland Barthes perceives in *Writing Below Zero* (1953), literature is already a posthumous affair. Again, Nietzsche warns in the Foreword to *The Anti-Christ*, 'Only the day after tomorrow belongs to me. Some are born posthumously'.[25] The best one can do is realise a literature of perpetual deferral, challenging theology with those things which are too often excluded by its systematic claims – laughter, expenditure, meaninglessness, loss.[26] It is a challenge to the (almost) inevitable formalism of theological practice, not as blatant but still risking the offence of Georges Bataille's erotic prose, for somehow the scandal and the stumbling-block must be reintroduced to overturn the rhetorical machinery of religious power. And so, Bataille proclaims in his Preface to his novella *Madame Edwarda* (1956):

> At the further end of this pathetic meditation – which, with a cry, undoes itself, unravelling to drown in self-repudiation, for it is unbearable to its own self – we rediscover God. That is the meaning, that is the enormity of this *insensate* – this mad – book: a book which leads God upon the stage, God in the plenitude of His

attribution; and this God, for all that, is what? A public whore, in no way different from any other public whore. But what mysticism could not say (at the moment it began to pronounce its message, it entered it – entered its trance), eroticism does say: God is nothing if He is not, in every sense, the surpassing of God . . .[27]

Bataille, like his precursor Søren Kierkegaard – the supreme ironist – continually leads one to the brink of, and beyond, the acceptable, each writer being essentially poetic and unphilosophical. The community is freed, even if unwillingly, from the deception which denies it the freedom which it fears.[28] Derrida perceives Bataille's text as 'in the initial sense of the word, a *scandal*',[29] and it is Bataille's excess which makes him so dangerous, and so necessary.

One may not want to read much of the fiction of Bataille entering as much of it does into the realm of pornography. But as a thinker and creative writer at least he shakes us out of our textual complacency – our sense that certain texts are safe or even salvific, because they are about 'nice' things, and because they have the effect of reassuring, of consoling, while all the time they are effectively controlling us in our brave new world. What is needed is a more daring and a more radical concept of textuality which will overturn our expectations and securities, a genuine 'theological' text which is, in Robert Scharlemann's words, 'a religious or ontological text that is overturned so as not to be what it is or to be what it is not'.[30] The implications of this comment in the work of Scharlemann are explored at length in Chapter 8.

The fabric of these introductory pages, as of the whole book, is an inter-weaving of textual references from both within and intertextually. Such a fabric should challenge and strengthen the reader, its indirection and reserve a means of freedom from the domination of textual power which effects control by the establishment of apparently clear meaning and the tendency to doctrinal orthodoxy.

For life is not like that. A recent textbook on rhetoric, Walter Nash's *Rhetoric: The Wit of Persuasion* (1989), claims to 'rehabilitate rhetoric' as an ordinary human competence',[31] yet in its defence of rhetoric in the tradition of the (dubious) 'social practice'[32] of Aristotle and Cicero it leaves this reader at least uncomfortably aware of the designs of the argument upon him.

Yet Nash, being a good rhetorician, does not present his book as an argument. Rhetoric does not depend upon argumentation, and ultimately tends to leave you no options, for one must either believe or be damned. Is it a bad rhetoric – or a very subtle art of persuasion indeed – which deliberately invites disagreement, disapproval, academic censure? How far does the irony extend, in a text like the present which admits a fascination with the business of irony? Let the reader understand for himself, and at least begin to question the possibility of theology and theological discourse once again in a world in which divine hilarity alone may survive the inevitable death of the God who is apparently sustained by the rhetoric of our sacred texts, liturgy and literature.

Notes

1. Ivan Klíma, *My First Loves*. Trans. Ewald Osers (Harmondsworth, 1989) p. 89.
2. See, Michel Foucault, 'Truth and Power', in *Power/Knowledge. Selected Interviews and other Writings. 1972–77*. Ed. Colin Gordon (New York, 1980) pp. 109–33, esp. pp. 132–3.
3. For a detailed discussion see, Milan Kundera, *The Art of the Novel*. Trans. Linda Asher (London, 1988) pp. 158–65.
4. Some obvious places for the English reader to start would be: Peter Dixon, *Rhetoric* (London, 1971); George A. Kennedy, *Classical Rhetoric and its Christian and Secular Tradition from Ancient to Modern Times* (Chapel Hill, 1980); Walter Nash, *Rhetoric. The Wit of Persuasion* (Oxford, 1989); Brian Vickers, *In Defence of Rhetoric* (Oxford, 1988); Chaim Perelman, *The Realm of Rhetoric*. Trans. William Kluback (Notre Dame, 1982). All these books will be referred to repeatedly throughout this study.
5. See, Stanley Fish, 'Rhetoric', in *Doing What Comes Naturally* (Durham, NC, 1989) pp. 471–502, esp. pp. 492–3.

6. The point is derived from Derrida's much misunderstood aphorism, 'There is nothing outside of the text'. *Of Grammatology*. Trans. Gayatri Chakravorty Spivak (Baltimore, 1976), p. 158. See also, Kevin Hart, *The Trespass of the Sign. Deconstruction, Theology and Philosophy* (Cambridge, 1989) pp. 25–6.
7. Paul de Man, *Allegories of Reading* (Yale, 1979) p. 10, and passim.
8. Ibid. p. 113.
9. Here I am indebted to Terry Eagleton's essay 'J.L. Austin and the Book of Jonah', in Regina Schwartz (Ed.), *The Book and the Text. The Bible and Literary Theory* (Oxford, 1990) pp. 234–6. Also, de Man, op. cit. pp. 121 ff.
10. Eagleton, ibid. p. 234.
11. Ibid. p. 236.
12. Foucault, op. cit. p. 122.
13. S.T. Coleridge writing on Christianity, in *Aids to Reflection* 1825 (London, 1913) p. 134.
14. F. Nietzsche, *Twilight of the Idols* 1889. Trans. R.J. Hollingdale (Harmondsworth, 1990) p. 41.
15. Ibid. p. 44.
16. Jean-François Lyotard, *The Postmodern Condition: A Report on Knowledge*. Trans. Geoff Bennington and Brian Massumi (Manchester, 1984) p. 81.
17. *Twilight of the Idols*. p. 84.
18. See also, Acts of the Apostles 4: 11.
19. F. Nietzsche, *The Anti-Christ* 1895. Trans. R.J. Hollingdale (Harmondsworth, 1990) p. 165.
20. Ibid. p. 167.
21. Arthur Evans, *The God of Ecstasy. Sex Roles and the Madness of Dionysos* (New York, 1988) p. 169.
22. See, R.D. Stock, *The Flutes of Dionysus. Demonic Enthrallment in Literature* (Nebraska, 1989), Epilogue: 'Goatfoot Jesus?' pp. 401–8.
23. See, Evans, op. cit. p. 172 and Wilfred Schoff, 'Tammuz, Pan and Christ'. *The Open Court*, v. 39 (1912) 513–32.
24. Evans, op. cit. p. 173.
25. *The Anti-Christ* p. 124.
26. See also, Mark C. Taylor's discussion of Georges Bataille in his *Deconstruction in Context* (Chicago, 1986) p. 28.
27. Georges Bataille, Preface to *Madame Edwarda* 1956. Trans. Austryn Swainhouse (London, New York, 1989) pp. 141–2.
28. Compare, Dostoyevsky, 'The Grand Inquisitor': 'They will marvel at us and they will regard us as gods because, having become their masters, we consented to endure freedom and rule over them – so dreadful will freedom become to them in the end!' *The Brothers Karamazov* 1880. Trans. David Magarshack (Penguin, 1958) Vol. I p. 297. Erich Fromm, also, in *Escape from Freedom* (New York, 1941), examines the fear of freedom, and the social and psychological attractions of totalitarian movements.
29. Jacques Derrida, *Writing and Difference*. Trans. A. Bass (Chicago, 1978) p. 268.

30. Robert P. Scharlemann, *Inscriptions and Reflections, Essays in Philo-sophical Theology* (Charlottesville, 1989) p. 57. See also Scharlemann's forthcoming paper 'Textuality between Theology and Literature', to be published in a volume on the work of Paul Ricoeur. Ed. David Klemm.
31. Walter Nash, *Rhetoric: The Wit of Persuasion* (Oxford, 1989) p. ix.
32. Ibid., p. 218.

2

Plato, Rhetoric and Community: Lethal Persuasions

It is evident how much men love to deceive and to be deceived, since rhetoric, that powerful instrument of error and deceit, has its established professors, is publicly taught, and has always been had in great reputation: and I doubt not but it will thought great boldness, if not brutality, in me to have said thus much against it. Eloquence, like the fairer sex, has too prevailing beauties in it to suffer itself ever to be spoken against. And it is in vain to find fault with those arts of deceiving, wherein men find pleasure to be deceived.[1]

John Locke, in his *Essay Concerning Human Understanding* (1690), blissfully unaware of the sensitivities of feminist criticism, provides a rhetorical starting-point for the concerns of my present enquiry. In the previous chapter I applied Foucault's description of the phenomena of power in the state to the church. Equally, Locke's presentation of rhetoric, as the powerful art of persuasion, can so easily be recategorised as a portrait of religion, or the institution of at least the Christian tradition, which is the church. For the church, too, has its established professors and confessors, is publicly taught in text, sermon and liturgy, and has always been held, by an appreciable number of people, in great reputation. No doubt there will be those who consider some of my writing to be of great boldness, if not brutality towards their perceived notion of the Christian tradition. I must take my chance:

the blandishments of rhetoric, like those of religion, may prove too seductive. But, if nothing else, each chapter of this book is an exercise in rhetoric, and the reader must decide for herself whether she is persuaded by an argument, or whether there is a deeper purpose running counter to any demonstrable claims. Irony can be a useful tool for and against the rhetorician.

Maurice Blanchot, in *L'Entretien infini* (1969), writes of the difficulty of approaching the language of Heraclitus,[2] a language which, Blanchot suggests, pre-dates our linguistic dualism and is remote from us in vocabulary, semantics and, above all, its sense of signification.[3] An untranslatable language, in remote purity, it is succeeded by the language of Plato and Aristotle with its arbitrary association of *signifiant* and *signifié,* and by the moment when translation becomes not only possible, but necessary. That moment is occupied pre-eminently by Socrates – not the 'real' Socrates, but Plato's myth – 'constituting the brightness that creates the darkness around and beyond him'.[4] In the art of translation, which recognises the fluctuating, mischievous contrivances of grammar and syntax and the impossibility of wholly grasping them, Socrates pursues his calling, moving not from language to language, but rhetorically within ideas, introducing (as Kierkegaard knew so well[5]) irony into the world. Typically, Phaedrus is perplexed by Socrates' assertions:

ΦΑΙ : Ἐῖεν οὕτω δὴ δοκεῖ παίζειν;
ΣΩ : Δοκῶ γάρ σοι παίζειν καὶ οὐχὶ ἐσπουδακέναι;

(Phaedrus: Do you think that this is a laughing matter? Socrates: Why, don't you think I'm serious?)

One can never trust the word of an ironist, in whose hands the weaker can seem stronger and truth unstable, though argument powerful.

Translating Blanchot's *Thomas L'obsur* (1941) is a supremely rhetorical exercise, since the translation, like rhetoric itself, completely devours its object, though whether the cause of that is the object itself one can never quite be sure. Robert Lamberton, Blanchot's translator, reflected upon what Blanchot might think of his efforts:

> In the absence of any concrete evidence, I imagine the author of the works of Maurice Blanchot responding to the idea, the fact of the translation of his work (whether mine or another) with that 'Nietzschean hilarity' Jeffrey Mehlman sees as characteristic of him – the dialectical twin of the austerity of his prose – and that this imaginary confrontation might be summed up in a phrase from *Celui qui ne m'accompagnait pas* equally evoked by Mehlman: 'This gaiety passed into the space I thought I occupied and dispersed me' ('Orphée scripteur', *Poétique* 20 [1974]).[7]

This hilarity, it may be said, will be heard throughout the present work, an examination of religious rhetoric and an exercise in rhetoric which may either persuade (one way or another) or leave the reader a little more wary, usefully uncertain.

We should at this stage consider in some detail the nature and purpose of rhetoric in the classical tradition. Although Erich Auerbach, and after him G.B. Caird, have sought to distinguish the New Testament writings from the spirit of classical rhetoric,[8] I rest my discussion here upon the universality of Aristotle's purpose in writing the *Rhetoric*, to describe a phenomenon which is a universal facet of human experience.[9] And in what I shall argue in subsequent chapters, though the terms may remain to a certain extent those of classical rhetoric, their use may be radically adapted as rhetorical criticism of the texts of the New Testament, and the religious tradition is recognised as the necessary, indeed vital, counterpart of hermeneutics as enquiry, not only into the art of understanding and appropriating meaning, but into the very fundamental questions of theology itself.[10]

'ῥήτωρ' might be defined as 'a man skilled in speaking who addresses a public audience in order to make an impact upon it';[11] 'rhetoric' as 'argumentative composition',[12] 'that quality in discourse by which a speaker or writer seeks to accomplish his purposes',[13] or 'reflection on the role of style in the art of persuasion'.[14] Aristotle, we may recall, distinguished three categories in the arts of language: logic, rhetoric and poetic. Very briefly, 'clarity' and the ability to persuade and change our opinions are the functions of logic and rhetoric. Poetic, on the other hand, has 'distinctiveness' rather than 'clarity', and by moving beyond the realms of 'ordinary' speech, does not seek so much to persuade as to invite us to use our imaginations.[15]

In short, rhetoric is concerned with persuasion, power and authority. Even in Wayne Booth's classic study *The Rhetoric of Fiction* (1961), which avowedly ignores 'fiction used for propaganda or instruction', the criticism is concerned to explore 'the author's means of controlling his reader'.[16] By rhetorical means and 'invention' – the treatment of the subject matter, the use of evidence, the argumentation, and the control of emotion – power is asserted which establishes a situation, or changes it, and in the relating of form and content in, for example, a biblical text, it is the creative synthesis of the specific formulation with the content of a pericope that makes it a distinctive and powerful composition.[17] It should be clear, therefore, why classical rhetoricians were so insistent that goodness is a necessary prerequisite of the true orator.[18] Never far away is the anxiety that rhetoric may be used by the wicked man as a tool for manipulation to his own evil ends. And, yet more disturbingly, in Plato's *Gorgias* and *Phaedrus*, we move nearer to the suspicion that the evil lies in rhetoric itself – a vaunted art of deception, a contrivance and falsification of great power. Indifferent to truth and morality, rhetoric must be subordinated according to Plato, or so it would appear, to dialectic, whose province is definition and division in the ceaseless search for truth.

Against this subordination and in defence of rhetoric, Aristotle makes his counter-claim in the very opening sentence of the *Rhetoric*: 'Rhetoric is the counterpart (ἀντίστροφος) of dialectic. Both alike are concerned with such things as come, more or less, within the general ken of all men and belong to no definite science'.[19] The two studies, in other words, fit together, each the legitimate equal of the other in discipline and intellectual rigour. But did I say Aristotle? Or did I mean St Paul? Indeed, following William Spooner, one may wish to say that 'In the sermon which I have just completed, wherever I said Aristotle, I meant St Paul.' For it is my contention that in the New Testament we have erred grievously in our failure to heed Socrates and his warnings against rhetoric, since in the New Testament, so obsessed with theology, we are playing with power in the ultimate degree, and rhetoric is in its element, playing its subtle games with a freedom that eludes authorial or even rational demands.

Since Aristotle, nevertheless, rhetoric has always had its defenders among those who would claim for it a role higher and more elevated than that of mere persuasion. To persuade one to be good and true is a noble thing, always assuming that goodness and truth are stable commodities and acceptable universal currency. But one may be persuaded by powerful argument or beautiful words to believe that which is less than honest or to do that which contributes nothing to a neighbour's welfare. Rhetoric – the manipulation of the dualisms and the dislocations of language – is a weapon of power in the constitution and control of communities, and never more radically so than when communities claim to embody and represent the highest good. For such religious communities depend upon essential and constitutive qualities – truth, goodness, beauty – and the antiessentialism which underlies rhetorical thinking feeds upon this dependency, and is a canker most closely at the heart of the most authoritative religious and theological claims. Ironically, theology may have to rediscover itself in the Western tradition through the terms of someone like Richard Rorty, that most anti-theological of neo-pragmatists, who has most shrewdly chronicled our epistemological condition and its limitations. In this portrait of truth I have deliberately avoided the category of truth as Being as described by Plotinus. According to Rorty:

> There . . . are two ways of thinking about various things . . . The first . . . thinks of truth as vertical relationship between representations and what is represented. The second . . . thinks of truth horizontally – as the culminating reinterpretation of our predecessors' reinterpretation of their predecessors' reinterpretation . . . It is the difference between regarding truth, goodness and beauty as external objects which we try to locate and reveal, and regarding them as artifacts whose fundamental design we often have to alter.[20]

The second, it seems to me, recognises the Socratic moment in language with a sense of realism that shatters Heraclitean linguistic wholeness, and it is through this door that we shall need to go to recover theological thinking, a new Platonism via a Platonic suspicion of rhetoric.

There is good reason to be unprofessional and avoid Aristotle, for whom, in the *Rhetoric*, the rhetorical faculty is not in itself inclined to abuse the truth. On the contrary, he prefers to suggest that 'other things affect the result considerably, owing to the defects of our hearers' (III, 1404, see below p. 49). To put this more cynically, you have only got yourself to blame. Rhetoric, indeed, according to Aristotle, is simply anxious to get at the facts:

We must be able to employ persuasion, just as strict reasoning can be employed, on opposite sides of a question, not in order that we may in practice employ it in both ways (for we must not make people believe what is wrong), but in order that we may see clearly what the facts are.[21]

If, then, rhetoric is a heuristic to enable us to discover the facts, the moral tone of Aristotle at this point is, to say the least, ambiguous. Praxis allows the ambiguity, while the moral imperative drives us towards the truth. But need that be so? Persuasion can work both ways, eschewing essentialist adherence to particular values.

Equally, it may be that for Plato, a 'true rhetoric' must be based on knowledge of the eternal realities,[22] but ironically within the dialogue, truth itself becomes a rhetorical term, defined, like all such terms, as neither good or bad, but enabling 'the argument to proceed with clearness and consistency'. (*Phaedrus* 265 d 5)

As Brian Vickers has demonstrated in his book *In Defence of Rhetoric* (1988), Plato's critique of rhetoric in the *Phaedrus* is reforming as well as destructive. In Vickers' words:

To posterity Plato has more often seemed the out-and-out enemy of rhetoric, greeted or scorned accordingly. Yet his immediate impact within the Academy was constructive. His pupil Aristotle began lecturing on rhetoric before Plato's death, evidently with his Master's approval, and in lectures extending over a period of years both expanded Plato's positive suggestions and refuted some of his attacks.[23]

Vickers' argument for the Platonic reform of rhetoric, however, is oddly naive, true only in the terms of rhetorical truth. For Socrates ironically illustrates that rhetoric works with most constructive impact when, as the art of persuasion, it is most truly itself, constituting its own terms.

'Can it be', asks Socrates of Phaedrus, 'that what I have been describing is precisely that art of rhetoric to which Thrasymachus and the rest owe their ability not only to speak themselves, but to make a good speaker of anyone who is prepared to pay them tribute as if they were kings?'[24] By his own confession, Socrates joins the ranks of Thrasymachus of Chalcedon (in the *Republic*) and Callicles (in the *Gorgias*) who maintain by their rhetoric that Might is Right.

It is a lethal persuasion, establishing all within its own terms. A reading of the *Phaedrus* takes one into and beyond Stanley Fish's notion of a self-consuming artifact, to that intimidation which thrives on the very suggestion of reformation and the achievement of meaning. As Roland Barthes has expressed it, in such writing there is contained 'the ambiguity of an object which is both language and coercion: there exists fundamentally in writing a "circumstance" foreign to language, there is, as it were, the weight of a gaze conveying an intention which is no longer linguistic'.[25]

The circumstance of rhetoric is death, shining 'with its maximum brilliance when it attempts to die'. For there is, in fact, nothing outside the linguisticality of Socratic irony beyond the one absolute assumption that enables us to say that we are alive; that is, that we shall die. Literature becomes, then, a posthumous affair, while the most powerful arts of persuasion are those which convince us that dying we live, that there is life within the sacred text and from its very textuality is intimated an intention which is no longer of language. The Pauline epistles exploit masterfully this 'circumstance' within the powerful formalism of their rhetorical textuality, faith coming from what is heard (Romans 10: 17). Indeed at the conclusion of the Bible itself, the future promise is generated only from within the textuality of what 'He who gives this testimony speaks. "Yes, I am coming soon!"' (Revelation 22: 20). In the passion of language is always a possible threat of retribution, in which (in Barthes' words) 'the

alibi stemming from language is at the same time intimidation and glorification; for it is power of conflict which
produces the purest types of writing'.[26]

To return, then, to the *Phaedrus*. Wherein is located the
power of its persuasion? Here, and elsewhere, Plato describes human life as a declension from a higher state, our
efforts on earth as attempts to recover a lost vision. Our
version of reality, suggested by the senses, is inevitably
partial and distorted, and must be overturned in an
inversion which involves an ironic assessment of
rationality, a dialectical examination of things as they are
perceived. This dialectic is supremely operative in the
Phaedrus. To regard it therefore as the exposing of rhetoric in all its shallowness and inconsistency[27] in the face
of substantial dialectic, is entirely to miss the point that
the dialogue is, in Fish's words, 'a series of discrete
conversations or seminars, each with its own carefully
posed question, ensuing discussion, and firmly drawn
conclusion; but so arranged that to enter into the spirit
and assumptions of any one of these self-enclosed units
is implicitly to reject the spirit and assumptions of the
unit immediately preceding'.[28]

Fish's observation is crucial. For in apparently demo-
lishing rhetoric, Socrates is actually the consummate
rhetorician, playing to the full the rhetorical game of
binding everything within the terms of the rhetoric which,
in self-denial, becomes most powerful. For the rhetorical
world is entirely self-enclosed, establishing the terms of
its own morality and assumptions – in Derrida's now
familiar words in *Of Grammatology* (1974), there is
nothing outside of the text. There is only the larger,
ever-receding textuality of the Socratic myth (and like
Socrates, Jesus Christ never actually wrote anything himself) making the power of the unwritten 'dominical' words
yet more powerful in writing which is rhetorically–
hermeneutically infinitely expansive. Is there any real
difference between our response to Socratic irony and the

fear of the disciples in St Mark's Gospel?) Here is Socrates in action. He asks Phaedrus:

> . . . if a speech is to be classed as excellent, does not that presuppose knowledge of the truth about the subject of the speech in the mind of the speaker?[29]

Phaedrus disagrees, suggesting that rhetorical skill has nothing to do with the truth but 'what is likely to seem right in the eyes of the mass of people who are going to pass judgement'. But Socrates persists, and argues that this kind of pragmatic position, which so easily ends up 'by representing evil as in fact good' reaps a very un-satisfactory harvest. It will simply be undone by its own self-evident absurdities. Phaedrus agrees.

Then, however, Socrates changes his ground almost imperceptibly. For truth is reserved only for the rhetor-ician himself, a mysterious quality which he may have no intention of sharing with his listeners. Truth and rhetoric are indissoluble, but what is truth? – a question always to be asked of the, finally silent, orator. Socrates maintains to Phaedrus:

> . . . a man who sets out to mislead without being misled himself must have an exact knowledge of the likenesses and unlikenesses between things . . . Is it possible for a man to be skilled in leading the minds of his hearers by small gradations of difference in any given instance from truth to its opposite, or to escape being misled himself, unless he is acquainted with the true nature of the thing in question?

Phaedrus is convinced, but by now the ground has shifted almost completely. Knowledge of the truth is indeed essential for the orator, but rhetoric, in remaining true *to itself* can consume even itself in a massive instability which the hearer perceives only as power. A supreme example of such persuasion is the dialogue between Jesus and Pilate in St John's Gospel 18: 33–8. Like Socrates with Phaedrus, Jesus knocks away every rung of the ladder beneath Pilate's feet, so that when by implication, he is faced with the truth (rhetoric and truth being one), he has no idea of the truth (the irony being perfected), and is rendered totally powerless. '"For my part", he said, "I find no case against him"' (18: 38). The whole of the Gospel, indeed, like the *Phaedrus*, is a series of rhetorical artifacts, each disconfirming – and according to rhetorical truth, therefore, powerfully confirming – its predecessors, until the final great ambiguity, the cry from the cross, an untranslatable Greek word, 'τετέλεσται' ('it is accomplished') (19: 30).

The *Phaedrus* beautifully inscribes in its argument the power of the rhetoric which stabilises our inadequacies and limitations. It traps us in the dangers that it warns us of and rhetorically undoes Aristotelian defences of rhetoric. From whence comes its power? From nothing but language itself, and the slippages within language in its deliberate ironic play of intertextuality. In the self-consuming, deconstructive interplay of the Socratic dialogue, the rhetoric gains its justification and its textual purity developed by conflict and in the exercise of power: such purity both threatens and glorifies.[30]

In this linguistic celebration is motivated what the literary critic and comparatist Mieke Bal has described as 'the ever-dynamic meaning'[31] to present itself as fixed, an illusion that encourages the appearance of dialogue and debate. Hermeneutics arise out of the felt need to interpret continually from this assumed base – the foundation of all creeds and doctrines – but inherent in the hermeneutic process is failure as negotiations are Socratically disconfirmed. What is truth? There is no truth when the critical dimension is located in failure. In Mieke Bal's words:

The excess or lack of arguments points to the attempt to impose meaning; hence, they signify force. Failure, then, becomes the model speech-act that displays the anchorage of meaning within the motivating force and the enactment of the attempt that fails. As Felman writes, 'Failure refers not to an absence, but to the enactment of a difference'.[32]

This may be illustrated from an example of biblical intertextuality. The story of the near-sacrifice of Isaac in Genesis 22 is familiar enough. Its intertextual relationship with the less well-known sacrifice of the anonymous daughter of Jephthah in Judges 11: 29–40 has been examined by Elaine Scarry and Mieke Bal.[33] Difference there certainly is between the two 'sacrifices'. In the girl's case there is no love for the daughter at stake, and the sacrifice is actually carried out ('he fulfilled the vow he made', v. 39). More remarkable are the similarities; the exile to the mountain wilderness, the behaviour of the fathers in the face of God. What is so appalling in narrative terms is the vividness with which the scene of Isaac's *non*-sacrifice is described (classically examined by Erich Auerbach in *Mimesis* (1946)), and the minimal representation of the enacted sacrifice in Judges.

> At the end of two months she came back to her father, and he fulfilled the vow he had made; she died a virgin. (11: 39)

The radical sense of ritual violence is barely depicted: the non-event of Isaac's 'sacrifice', so often the subject of artists and painters, is celebrated as an instance of God's mercy – the same God who demanded that Jephthah keep his vow. It is the difference which matters. The restoration of Isaac (a sacrificial *mistake*) lives in religious history, while the routine ritual murder of Jephthah's daughter is taken for granted, commemorated merely liturgically by the daughters of Israel four days a year (Judges 11: 40).

It is a stark instance of how religious rhetoric works. The text, as self-consuming artifact, valorises the exception, while almost tacitly endorsing the rule of violence, the violence which subdues, intimidates and (perhaps) glorifies. This violence is present in the frightened community of St Mark's Gospel, and only occasionally, under great stress, does the poet dare to ruin the sacred 'truths'[34] and expose the vicious rhetoric underlying the Abraham/ Isaac story of God's mercy. Thus wrote Wilfrid Owen, from the trenches of the Great War:

The Parable of the Old Man and the Young

So Abram rose, and clave the wood, and went,
And took the fire with him, and a knife,
And as they sojourned both of them together,
Isaac the first-born spake and said, My Father,
Behold the preparations, fire and iron,
But where the lamb for this burnt-offering?
Then Abram bound the youth with belts and straps,
And builded parapets and trenches there,
And stretched forth the knife to slay his son.
When lo! an angel called him out of heaven.
Saying, Lay not thy hand upon the lad,
Neither do anything to him. Behold,
A ram, caught in a thicket by the horns;
Offer the Ram of Pride instead of him.
But the old man would not so, but slew his son,
And half the seed of Europe, one by one.

The purity of ritual murder surfaces within the self-enclosed textuality of meaningless warfare, a liturgical rhetoric devoid of deity, under extreme pressure abandoning the seductive language of divine forgiveness in a final rejection of possibility.

What does theology do then? Rejoicing in failure (an excuse for grace) it slips back into the enactment of difference and serenely celebrates the liturgical death of Jephthah's daughter and her countless sisters. But not for Owen. While, as an officer, he was training men in England for war, and himself preparing to return to the trenches in July 1918, he wrote to Osbert Sitwell:

I see to it that he is dumb, and stands to attention before his accusers. With a piece of silver I buy him every day, and with maps make him familiar with the topography of Golgotha.[35]

Owen scandalises the careful intertextuality of religious rhetoric whose canonical, scriptual surface repeatedly displaces the faithful reader, subjecting her to the fearful obedience which the religious community demands.

Socratic irony in the *Phaedrus* beautifully embraces the conditions of religious rhetoric and the community which it sustains. How ironic is Kierkegaard when he exclaims, 'Dear reader! allow me but one sentence, one innocent parenthesis in order to express my gratitude for the solace I found in reading Plato. For where is one to find solace if not in that infinite calm wherein the idea, during the stillness of the night, silently, gracefully, yet so mightily unfolds itself in the rhythm of the dialogue as if nothing else in the world existed'.[36] Where but in the rhythm of the dialogue, in its embracing rhetoric? As the translator of Blanchot recognised (as of Joyce, Mallarmé or Nietzsche), translation moves from word, to phrase, to sentence, to paragraph to the entire work, each refusing to yield its integrity, each pointing provocatively to the 'bug-eyed monster' which the Platonist calls 'the eternal thought,'[37] and which makes its demands whether or not it exists. But nothing escapes the falsely prophetic text for there is nothing outside its irony, and for Plato, the myth of Socrates becomes ever more necessary as its relationship with the actual Socrates becomes more arbitrary. The greatest myths leave no writing, but inspire a powerful textuality, 'a kind of natural ambience wholly pervading the writer's expression, yet without endowing it with form or content: it is, as it were, an abstract circle of truths'.[38]

A community under the realm of rhetoric is bound most powerfully, therefore, when the textuality to which it continually refers yields to nothing but points to perpetually deferred/differing future. Nothing is abolished (irony abolishes nothing and wastes nothing), but completion is promised, and the promise demands total commitment under its condition of possible fulfilment. The ironic secret is to see the point, but the greatest irony flourishes in the darkness, unseen and unrecognised. Its comic nature is hard, indeed, to unravel. It was through faith (faith in what – the sacred truths of textuality?) that Jephthah, having successfully indulged in the ritual sacrifice of his daughter, 'overthrew kingdoms, established justice, saw God's promises fulfilled' (Hebrews 11: 32–3). According to the writer of the Epistle, he shared with all people of faith, a vision of the glory to come and its intimidation, and persuaded of such a promise, Jephthah could hardly withstand the demands of the present. Within the persuasion of his vow he is trapped, since persuasion cannot be circumvented or bottomed out. For it underwrites everything, being a part of the very effort taken to evade it. There is no final line.[39]

Nothing stands outside rhetoric. In the *Phaedrus*, the rhetorician may be seen as playing to the immediate desires of his audience, confirming the *status quo* ('Firmly I believe, and truly'), impeding moral progress and establishing criteria for judgement from within. 'The good' is that which is pragmatically satisfactory:

ΣΩ : Ἀτάρ, ὦ φίλε φαῖδρε, δοκῶ τι σοί, ὥσπερ
        ἐμαυτῷ, θεῖον πάθος πεπονθέναι;

ΦΑΙ : Πάνυ μὲν οὖν, ὦ Σώκρατες, παρὰ τὸ
          εἰωθὸς εὐροία τίς σε εἴληφεν.
ΣΩ : Σιγῇ τοίνυν μου ἄκουε.

(Socrates: Tell me, my dear Phaedrus, do you think, as
I do, that I am inspired?
Phaedrus: Undoubtedly you have been carried away
by a quite unusual flow of eloquence, Socrates.
Socrates: Be quiet then and listen).[40]

Socrates binds Phaedrus to himself with the phrase, 'do
you think, as I do?' The matter of his eloquence settled on
Socrates' terms, Phaedrus is reduced to obedient silence.
A biblical comparison immediately presents itself in the
Marcan account of the healing of the Gerasene demoniac
(Mark 5: 1–20) where Socrates' binding phrase δοκῶ τι
σοί, ὥσπερ ('Do you think, as I do?') is mirrored in the
demoniac's questions, τί ἐμοί καὶ ἐμαυτῷ σοί ('What have
you and I in common?'). The madman stands outside the
defining rhetoric of Jesus – demons are destroyed, in the
slaughter of the pigs, not drawn into the linguistic net of
persuasion. Pragmatism has more than one way of dealing with problems relating to the outsider.
    A splendid contemporary literary example of the *ironic*
outsider, the Socratic wit whose rhetoric mirrors, like
Socrates, its own assumptions, is found in Julian Barnes'
post-modern fiction *A History of the World in 10½ Chapters*
(1989). The scene is Noah's Ark, the archetypal
microcosmic world found in so many ships in literature –
in Herman Melville's *Billy Budd* or William Golding's *Rites
of Passage*. Each claim their sacrificial victim. Who is the
satirical narrator on board the Ark in Barnes' novel?
Certainly no stalwart member of the biblical shipboard
community:

    As far as we were concerned the whole business of the
    Voyage began when we were invited to report to a

certain place by a certain time. That was the first we
had heard of the scheme. We didn't know anything of
the political background. God's wrath with his own
creation was news to us; we just got caught up in it
willy nilly . . . I suppose it wasn't altogether Noah's
fault. I mean, that God of his was a really oppressive
role-model. Noah couldn't do anything without first
wondering what *He* would think. Now that 's no way
to go on. Always looking over your shoulder for
approval – it's not adult, is it?[41]

The narrator, after all, admits that it is not his fault that he
is a woodworm, lodged, a legitimate animal, in the
wooden Ark. Potentially destructive – or deconstructive
– of the whole enterprise, though remarkably self-
denying ('in a spirit of friendship' p. 25), the wormy
narrator reveals a remarkable insight into the nature of
the community, led and preserved as it is by Noah who,
the official history assures us, is alone righteous before
God in his generation (Genesis 7: 1).

The enterprise of the Ark in Barnes' narrative succeeds
by oppression and the preservation of its members in
ignorance. Utterly serious in its performance and effect,
the divine rhetoric thrives upon irony, an irony which
inevitably reflects back upon its perpetrator, since God is
finally bound to his own elect. 'Noah probably realised
he had God over a barrel (what an admission of failure to
pull the Flood and then be obliged to ditch your First
Family)' (p. 22). But the real irony is the woodworm, who
is a stowaway.

We had survived. We had stowed away, survived and
escaped – all without entering into any fishy covenants
with either God or Noah. We had done it by ourselves.
We felt enobled as a species. That might strike you as
comic, but we did: we felt enobled. (p. 28)

The divine comedy of the ironic outsider, beyond the religious community of sacred rhetoric, yet himself supremely rhetorical, is to be celebrated in his refusal to consume the artifact upon which his life depends. A truly gracious act.

But one finds few woodworms celebrated in the history of the Christian community. On the contrary, the history of theology takes itself and its God too seriously for that. In Kierkegaard's *Parable of the Confessor and the Penitent*, we perceive that:

> Philosophy relates to history as a confessor to the penitent, and like a confessor, it ought to have a supple and searching ear for the penitent's secrets; but after having listened to a full account of his confession, it must then be able to make this appear to the penitent as an 'other'. And as the penitent individual is able to rattle off the fateful events of his life chronologically, even recite them entertainingly, but cannot himself see through them, so history is able to proclaim with loud pathos the rich full life of the race, but must leave its explanation to the elder (philosophy). History can then experience the pleasant surprise that while at first it would almost disown its philosophic counterpart, it afterwards identifies itself with this conception of philosophy to such a degree that, finally, it would regard this as the essential truth, the other as mere experience.[42]

Kierkegaard's rhetoric is beautifully seductive, a seamless web of irony. In his parable – like all great parables, destabilising and disconcerting though finally captivating – philosophy plays the role of the Socratic rhetorician. History, that faithful handmaiden of biblical scholarship and Christian belief, in its very recounting of itself, so full of sin, is shriven as the truth of rhetoric conforms the richness of life to its structures and performances. Beside this great deception all else is mere appearance, a jumbled and incoherent, though entertaining, account of events.

History, then, is trapped by explanation, the parable a witty, self-consuming artifact which denies its own 'meaning' in the very pronunciation of it. Kierkegaard, Dostoyevsky, Kafka and Borges warn us in their parables, in the passionate encounter between despair and hope, but still the religious tradition takes its Scripture too seriously not as 'an art born of the laughter of God',[43] its great parables as allegories or moral exempla and not as overturnings of the ontological; parables of the kingdom in which the kingdom of heaven is the kingdom of heaven as what is not the kingdom of heaven.[44]

Socrates in Plato warned us about rhetoric, and demonstrated its power, as well as a way out, not through texts, but in a recognition of their textuality (that we must relate to them, not be duped or subdued by any claims to 'meaning'), but his warning has gone largely unheeded in theology. I began this chapter noting Maurice Blanchot's lament for the language of Heraclitus in our time of linguistic dualism, though in fact Christian rhetoric has preferred to generate belief under the assumed conditions of unity proposed by Cicero in *De Oratore*, a work of profound moral irresponsibility.[45] According to Cicero there is an inseparable connection between the subject matter (*res*) and the words (*verba*) which purport to convey it. It is precisely the assumed inseparability of this link which my present argument denies for dear life. But according to Cicero, as Peter Dixon summarises him, 'we cannot talk of expressing a thought in different words, for it will become a different (even if only a slightly different) thought in the process'. Students under Cicero are required to understand and exercise the totality of thought and word, *res* and *verba*, in a synthetic denial of linguistic freedom and undecidability.

Cicero's public orator would have been deeply distasteful to Socrates. He is a man of public leadership and responsibility with a duty to persuade and establish by proof that his case be true. His irresponsibility lies in the completeness of his claims and the formality of his processes, in the concept of the *officia oratoris*, the duties of the orator. The very trust commanded by the orator will tend to make one distrustful – for there is no room here for the riddling, decentering irony of the Socratic figure.

From Cicero and Quintilian, St Augustine derives his discussion of Christian eloquence in the fourth book of *De Doctrina Christiana*.[46] From classical concepts, he could establish systematically for theology (as Cranmer was to do for the English liturgy) the rhetoric of religion which is derived from the Bible, that is a radical rhetoric[47] which is proclaimed rather than argued on the basis of probability, a rhetoric with a high authoritative claim which tends to disallow rational argument or disagreement: a powerful instrument for coercion, to impose conformity. The parliamentary guarantee for the English liturgy, in an act of conformity, in fact emerges also from within the rhetoric of the liturgy itself and its use within the worshipping community. This is discussed in detail in Chapter 5.

What has an Athenian, post-modern rhetoric to do with the Jerusalem of religious orthodoxy? The latter, it seems to me, always demands 'warrants of assent',[48] a commitment to a particular notion of the nature of things, a bringing of issues 'into perspective'.[49] A modern defender of rhetoric, Walter Nash, while bowing to pragmatics ('what is it we evaluate?'), is firmly committed, with Aristotle and Cicero, to the social practice of rhetoric whereby certainty may be engendered on the grounds of 'truthful' assumptions. Does rhetoric promote the possibility of an ontological argument?

If one still maintains any concern for a religious tradition – say, Christianity – it is, perhaps, too late (or too early) to demand or claim commitment, but one needs to ascertain once again whether it is meaningful, in any sense, to speak of a relationship between existence – however that is understood, and Christianity – however that is projected. Here we are back with Kierkegaard, in the fear and trembling of lying and utterance, and the insight that, if there *is* a relationship between existence and Christianity it is utterly and properly undecidable in terms of any immediate presentation.[50]

In a chapter which has, it may be, done little more than throw out feelers towards later discussions in this book, in Bakhtinian fragments of language deconstructively at war with one another on the ironic plain, I conclude with the inconclusive concluding words of Stanley Fish in his book *Self-Consuming Artifacts* (1972):

> . . . the theory, both as an account of meaning and as a way of teaching, is full of holes; and there is one great big hole right in the middle of it, which is filled, if it is filled at all, by what happens inside the user-student. The method, then, remains faithful to its principles, it has no point of termination; it is a process; it talks about experience and is an experience; its focus is effects and its result is an effect.[51]

(The reader who knows Fish's book will immediately comment that I have omitted the final sentence of his concluding paragraph. That may, or may not, matter. But like all rhetoricians who follow Socrates, I have taken a risk that at least the majority of people will not have perceived the way in which the truth has been used economically to serve a particular end.) The end is to subvert the conclusive tendencies of the art of persuasion, which may itself tend to powerful conclusions, like all postmodernist writing. A new beginning for theology, or a new desolation? ὁ ἀναγινώσκων νοείτω – let the reader understand. (Mark 13: 14).

Notes

1. John Locke, *An Essay Concerning Human Understanding*. Book III, Chap. 10. 1690. Repr. Dover Publications (New York, 1959) Vol. II pp. 146–7.
2. Maurice Blanchot, *L'Entretien infini* (Paris, 1969) pp. 119–20.
3. See Robert Lamberton, 'Thomas and the Possibility of Translation', in Blanchot, *Thomas l'Obscur*. Trans. Lamberton (New York, 1988) pp. 119–24.
4. Ibid. p. 120.
5. See, Søren Kierkegaard, *The Concept of Irony: with constant reference to Socrates* 1841. Trans. Lee M. Capel (London, 1966).
6. Plato, *Phaedrus* 234 d. 7–8. Trans. Walter Hamilton (Harmondsworth, 1973) p. 31.
7. Lamberton, op. cit. p. 121.
8. Erich Auerbach, *Mimesis*. Trans. Willard R. Trask (Princeton, 1968) pp. 39 ff. G.B. Caird, *The Language and Imagery of the Bible* (London, 1980) pp. 183–4.
9. See, George A. Kennedy, *New Testament Interpretation through Rhetorical Criticism* (Chapel Hill, 1984) pp. 10–11.
10. See, David E. Klemm, 'Towards a Rhetoric of Postmodern Theology: Through Barth and Heidegger'. *Journal of the American Academy of Religion* LV (1987) 443–69.
11. Peter Dixon, *Rhetoric* (London, 1971) p. 2.
12. Richard Whately, *Elements of Rhetoric*. 4th Edn. (Oxford, 1832) p. 6.
13. Kennedy, op. cit. p. 3.
14. Klemm, op. cit. p. 443.
15. See further, David Jasper, *The New Testament and the Literary Imagination* (London, 1987) pp. 30–1.
16. Wayne C. Booth, *The Rhetoric of Fiction* (Chicago and London, 1969). Preface.
17. See also, James Muilenburg, 'Form Criticism and Beyond'. *Journal of Literature* 88 (1969) 5. In this article, Muilenburg proposes a 'rhetorical criticism' as the next stage in consolidating the advantages and overcoming the deficiencies of form criticism.
18. See, Dixon, op. cit. pp. 4 ff.
19. Aristotle, *Rhetoric*. Trans. W. Rhys Roberts. *The Complete Works*. Vol. II. (Princeton, 1984) p. 2152.
20. Richard Rorty, *Consequences of Pragmatism* (Minneapolis, 1982) p. 92. See also, Stanley Fish, *Doing What Comes Naturally* (Duke, 1989) pp. 501–2.
21. Aristotle, *Rhetoric* I, 1355, 28–33. Quoted in Fish, op. cit. p. 479.
22. See Plato, *Phaedrus*. Translation, p. 79.
23. Brian Vickers, *In Defence of Rhetoric* (Oxford, 1988) p. 18.
24. *Phaedrus*, 266. Trans. p. 82.
25. Roland Barthes, *Writing Degree Zero* (1953), in Susan Sontag, *Barthes Selected Writings* (Fontana, 1983) p. 38.
26. Ibid. p. 39.

27. As in, Peter Dixon, *Rhetoric* (London, 1971) pp. 10–13.
28. Stanley Fish, *Self-Consuming Artifacts* (Los Angeles and London, 1972) p. 9.
29. *Phaedrus*, 259. Trans. p. 71. The following argument is taken from 259–62 of the dialogue, pp. 71–5. See also, Fish, *Self-Consuming Artifacts* pp. 10–12.
30. See above note 26.
31. Mieke Bal, *Death and Dissymmetry. The Politics of Coherence in the Book of Judges* (Chicago, 1988) p. 134.
32. Ibid. Quotation from Shashana Felman, *Le scandale du corps parlant* (Paris, 1980) p. 115.
33. Elaine Scarry, *The Body in Pain: The Making and Unmaking of the World* (New York, 1985) p. 204. Bal. op. cit. pp. 109–13.
34. See, Harold Bloom, *Ruin the Sacred Truths, Poetry and Belief from the Bible to the Present* (Harvard, 1989). The phrase is derived from Andrew Marvell's poem on *Paradise Lost*.
35. *The Collected Poems of Wilfrid Owen*. Ed. C. Day Lewis (London, 1963), Introduction p. 23.
36. Kierkegaard, *The Concept of Irony*. p. 65.
37. Robert Lamberton, op. cit. p. 122.
38. Roland Barthes, op. cit. p. 31.
39. See, Stanley Fish, 'Withholding the missing portion: power, meaning and persuasion in Freud's *The Wolf Man*', in Fabb, Athridge, Durant and MacCabe (Eds.), *The Linguistics of Writing* (Manchester, 1987) p. 170, and below, Chapter 7, pp. 105–6.
40. *Phaedrus* 238 c. 5–9. Translation, p. 37.
41. Julian Barnes, *A History of the World in $10\frac{1}{2}$ Chapters* (London, 1989) pp. 6, 21.
42. Kierkegaard, op. cit. p.48. See also Thomas C. Oden (Ed.), *Parables of Kierkegaard* (Princeton, 1989) p. 9.
43. Milan Kundera, *The Art of the Novel* (London, 1988). See also below, Chapter 9, pp. 136–40.
44. See, Robert P. Scharlemann, *Inscriptions and Reflections. Essays in Philosophical Theology*, p. 63. For a detailed discussion of this see below, Chapter 8, pp. 131–2.
45. For a brief description of Cicero's teaching, see Dixon, op. cit. pp. 15–18.
46. See, George A. Kennedy, *Classical Rhetoric and its Christian and Secular Tradition from Ancient to Modern Times* (Chapel Hill, 1980) p. 100.
47. See, Kennedy, *New Testament Interpretation Through Rhetorical Criticism* (Chapel Hill, 1984) pp. 6 ff. Kennedy's 'radical Christian rhetoric' is discussed in detail in Chapters 3 and 4.
48. Wayne C. Booth, *Modern Dogma and the Rhetoric of Assent* (Chicago, 1974) Chap. 4.
49. Walter Nash, *Rhetoric: The Wit of Persuasion* (Oxford, 1989) p. 218.
50. On this point, I am indebted to discussions with Professor Brayton Polka of York University, Toronto, Canada.
51. Fish, *Self-Consuming Artifacts* p. 426.

3

The Rhetoric of St Paul's Letters: Heaven Forbid!

Robert Scholes concludes his book *Textual Power* (1985) with these words:

> We care about texts for many reasons, not the least of which is that they bring us news that alters our way of interpreting things. If this were not the case, the Gospels and teachings of Karl Marx would have fallen upon deaf ears. Textual power is ultimately power to change the world.[1]

I want to add to these documents of power the further scriptural examples of the First and Second Letters of St Paul to the Thessalonians which are probably the earliest surviving written documents of the Christian tradition, and for that reason of particular interest. My brief examination of them will be through rhetorical criticism and in the manner which has already been outlined in the two preceding chapters, with the figure of the later Nietzsche lurking in the background. I.A. Richards, among others, as long ago as 1936, in his *Philosophy of Rhetoric* realised that 'rhetoric was too dangerous to be left to expire in peace',[2] and that literature is primarily a transaction between author and reader. Didactic and overtly persuasive writings in particular, therefore, require reassessment, and with the emergence of the so-called New Rhetoric under the scholarly guidance of Chaim Perelman and Mme L. Olbrechts-Tyteca, Plato's *Georgias* and *Phaedrus* have been increasingly subjected to the kind of pressure to which I have already subjected the latter in the previous chapter.

For Socrates in the *Phaedrus*, as we have seen, the very fixity of the written word is an obstacle in the path of truth, while rhetoric – unless subordinated to dialectic or perhaps the ironies of its own art – is a dangerous commodity, indifferent to truth and morality. Finally, and significantly for Socrates, rhetoric in the *Phaedrus* is only acceptable as an art when it is firmly based on the notion of truth inspired by love which is the common experience of 'true' philosophic activity.

If this is the case, and we follow as our guide Plato rather than Aristotle, the recent work of scholars of rhetoric like George Kennedy on the books of the New Testament is extremely problematic. For in his book *New Testament Interpretation Through Rhetorical Criticism* (1984), Professor Kennedy, acknowledging that New Testament writers wrote to persuade an audience of the truth of their messages, argues that these writers were employing rhetorical conventions that were widely known and practised in the Greek society of their times. More than this, Kennedy identifies what he calls a 'radical Christian rhetoric'[3] which draws not only upon Greek techniques but a scriptual inheritance from the Old Testament – that is the doctrine that the speaker is a vehicle of God's will. The essential rhetorical quality of the Old Testament is the assertion of God's authority, in that he has given his law to his people,[4] and the poet, speaker or orator claims the privilege of this authority as a mode of persuasion which depends very little, if at all, on logical argument. The Christian orator, in turn, claims to be a vehicle of God's will, prompted by God, and seeking to persuade not through the minds or understanding of his audience, but by the inspiration of divine love and grace which moves the heart. Thus St Paul writes in I Corinthians 2: 13, ' . . . we impart this in words not taught by human wisdom but taught by the Spirit, interpreting spiritual truths to those who possess the Spirit'.

Such spiritual truths must be, therefore, self-evident, and there is no way of arguing against what is self-evident,[5] for, properly, argumentation can intervene only where self-evidence is contested. Equally, however, it must be recognised that any *forms* of argumentation within such discourse may be powerful to create a particular disposition and claim validity even though its truth cannot necessarily and evidentially be established. Such argument is from authority rather than from demonstrable truth, and such authority – made respectable by the appearance of argumentation – might quickly claim the status of a self-evident spiritual truth in scripture. In Professor Perelman's words, 'the goal is always to strengthen a consensus around certain values which one wants to see prevail and which should orient action in the future'.[6]

Turning now to the writings of St Paul, and some recent critical work upon them, including that of George Kennedy, I find myself in some difficulty in the exercise of no little Socratic suspicion of rhetoric. Wilhelm Wuellner, in an article entitled 'Paul's Rhetoric of Argumentation in Romans' (1976) writes as follows:

My proposal is that a study of the rhetorical nature of Paul's argumentation, or a study of the argumentation in Paul's letters, will help us out of the two impasses created by the fixation with form- and genre-criticism on the one hand, and with specific social or political situations on the other hand. . . . I propose to replace the traditional priority on propositional theology and the more recent priority on letters as literature with the new priority on letters as argumentation. . . . I propose that in the rediscovery of the nature and purpose of argumentation as a basically rhetorical process we will find a more satisfactory way of accounting not only for the dialectical and logical dimensions, and for the literary dimensions in Paul's discourses, but also for the situational and social dimensions presupposed in Paul's letters (pp. 330–1).

These laudable proposals in the face of the generality of traditional Pauline scholarship rapidly begin to evaporate, however, as one realises time and again that what is presented by Paul as argument invariably gives a misleading impression. For example, in the familiar passage Romans 5: 18–21 on the first and second Adam, the style is clearly that of argument: 'it follows, therefore [Ἄρα οὖν]' (18): 'for as by [ὥσπεργὰρ] . . . thus also [οὕτως καὶ]' (19)ᵢ 'so that just as [ἵνα ὥσπερ] . . . thus also [οὕτως καὶ]' (21) [my translations]. The power of the writing, however, lies not in any logical development of thought, but actually from the excitement of a series of bold contrasts vigorously stated.[7] The same could also be said of the very similar style of I Corinthians 15: 35–58 on the resurrection of the dead.

The believer is thus dependent for her sense of reconciliation with God on nothing other than the robust assurance of the preacher that such is the case, and the style actually invalidates criticism of the preacher – his assurance is incontestable.

On the basis of this suggestion, I want to turn at more length now to the two early Pauline letters to the Thessalonians. I will not go into the details of scholarship concerning their date and authenticity. For various reasons it seems likely that the Thessalonian mission took place towards the end of 49 AD, the first letter being written early the following year, backed up by the second letter shortly afterwards. Some doubts have been expressed concerning the Pauline authorship of the second letter, but there seems no real reason to doubt the authenticity of both writings, and indeed as early as 120 AD Polycarp is quoting II Thessalonians as written by Paul.

We need, then, to ask what Paul was up to in 50 AD. The bulk of New Testament criticism has approached the literature from the general standpoint of 'form criticism', namely, to quote a standard work, C.F.D. Moule's *The Birth of the New Testament* (2nd Ed. 1966), 'that it is to the circumstances and needs of the worshipping, working, suffering community that one must look if one is to explain the genesis of Christian literature. Probably at no stage within the New Testament period did a writer put pen to paper without the incentive of a pressing need'.[8] For Professor Moule, what units the diversity of New Testament literature is unquestioned 'devotion to Jesus as Christ and Lord' (p. 10) and an acceptable, non-negotiable 'primacy of the divine initiative' (p. 211). Such critical presuppositions may even continue to be acceptable if one gladly adopts the rhetorical criticism of Kennedy and Wuellner. But when rhetoric itself begins to breed suspicion of the rhetorician in his use of discourse, in Perelman's words, 'to influence the intensity of an audience's adherence to certain theses'[9] one begins to be less charitably disposed towards St Paul than Professor Moule and even to suspect the bases upon which Christian theology itself has been so firmly settled – that divine initiative and authority which constitute an immensely powerful and over-serious instrument of communal control claiming the infallibility of dominical descent, a claim founded upon 'truth', which nevertheless may, in the actual terms of its rhetoric, be no more than a deception and the promotion of an absolute, abstract idea sustained within a carefully preserved myth.[10]

Pauline criticism has not properly recognised the implications of, on the one hand, Walter Ong's numerous discussions of the shift from orality to the technology of writing, or, on the other hand, reader-response examinations of the phenomenology of the reading process, particularly, perhaps, in the work of Wolfgang Iser.[11] That is, it has failed to admit the possibility that Paul (or his rhetoric) may be exploiting and manipulating the reader in the 'static spatial form' of a text which appears to create and sustain a freedom that is, in fact, illusory.

And, as Walter Wink has magisterially demonstrated in his multi-volume work *The Powers* (1984 ff), just as Paul is repeatedly anxious to unmask the idolatry of 'Sovereignties and Powers' (see, e.g. Ephesians 3: 10) in the language of power, so it may be that his sometimes violent rhetoric may constitute, in Wink's words, 'the direct use of power against a Power [which] will inevitably be to the advantage of The Powers That Be'.[12] Serious questions begin to arise about the very foundations of the Christian tradition and its theology in the exercise of such manipulative power.

Paul's First Letter to the Thessalonians is preoccupied with the assertion and exercise of the Apostle's authority. It opens collectively: 'Paul, Silvanus and Timothy, To the Church of the Thessalonians in God the Father and the Lord Jesus Christ'. (1: 1) Throughout the letter, however, and at crucial moments, Paul slips into the first person singular (2: 18, 5: 27), and repeatedly reminds his readers of their derivation from and dependence upon him:[13] 'And you became imitators (μιμηταὶ) of us and of the Lord' (1: 6); 'for you know how, like a father with his children, we exhorted each one of you' (2: 11): 'you learned from us how you ought to live' (4: 1). Paul thus leaves little space for mutuality or a real relationship between himself and the Thessalonians apart from that of their utter dependence upon him. Throughout the letter he emphasises the example which he sets, underwriting the pretense at argumentation with disarming claims of superiority. Since Paul claims that even his afflictions are divinely appointed, his prestige is actually increased by suffering and public humiliation (3: 4): a structure of reality is thus established in the text which effectively invalidates intellectual disagreement. It may be said that in building up his authority, Paul deserves to have his words believed.

But having effectively established his own position over against his readers, Paul gains greater effect by outright flattery of them, under the guise of prayer:

We give thanks to God always for you all, constantly mentioning you in our prayers, remembering before our God and Father your work of faith and labour of love and steadfastness of hope in our Lord Jesus Christ. (1: 2–3)

Indeed, the loyalty of the Thessalonian Christians constitutes Paul's authority and self-esteem – 'For you are our glory and joy' (2: 20). Not only, therefore, by flattery, but also by manipulation does he ensure its continuance. He offers freedom (5: 9, 5: 24) – but at a price, for his readers must 'lead a life worthy of God, who calls you into his own kingdom and glory' (2: 12). Such a life is actually dependent upon submission to Paul himself, and the promise of freedom is at the price of obedience to his authority.

If Paul does not actually confuse his authority with God's, he does not hesitate to insist, in the traditions of rhetoric, upon divine underwriting for his office, for, as he affirms, 'we have been approved by God to be entrusted with the gospel.' (2: 4). Anything which opposes his work is readily identified as Satanic (2: 18, 3: 5). Anything which displeases him, or threatens his authority – fornication and sexual license (4: 1 ff) or eschatological anxiety (5: 1 ff) – is flung back as an insult against God. 'Therefore whoever disregards this, disregards not man but God, who gives his Holy Spirit to you.' (4: 8).

The reader, therefore, is immediately placed at a disadvantage, since Christian privilege is entirely dependent upon Paul who engenders an atmosphere which is anxiously fearful of alienation. The good news of the gospel is presented not so much in terms of a present condition, but as a future reward (5: 9), and virtue is not its own reward. Instead, the Thessalonians are left in a state of nervous expectation which is a highly effective form of social control.

Finally, in addition to the weight of his own authority, Paul imposes on the Thessalonians the authority of their local leadership (5: 12–13). All in all, the heavy-handed tone of the letter is remarkably depressing, subordinating the reader by Paul's highly effective rhetorical strategy.

More briefly, the Second Letter to the Thessalonians is very similar. It seems quite clear that it was a follow-up to the first letter, an attempt to explain more clearly about Paul's teaching about the Parousia, the Second Coming. But Paul is even more insistent about his authorship of this letter, and the authority which that implies, for he concludes, presumably as a warning against forgeries: 'I, Paul, write this greeting with my own hand. This is the mark in every letter of mine; it is the way I write'. (3: 17).

It seems from this second letter that Paul's authority is being seriously threatened, and he asserts it by a subtle device, recognised by Perelman as well-tried in rhetoric, that is the claim to be speaking on higher authority. Paul begins by laying stress on his function as founder of the community and the source of their faith and belief (1: 10, 2: 5). Thus, the community's faith and trust in God is inextricably interwoven with their obedience to Paul: their religion, in effect, means doing what Paul tells them to do. For, despite his argumentative and disputatious stance, Paul recognises that the argument of rhetoric is from authority rather than from evident truth, and that controversy does not concern the argument itself, but the authority which presents it. Ultimately, furthermore, the only indisputable authority is divine authority, while within a community the 'competence' of its instrument must be recognised – in this case, Paul's status as an apostle (2: 14, 16; 3: 4, 6).[14]

It may be said, therefore, that Paul virtually identifies himself as the object of the Thessalonians' faith. Against his persecuting enemies he proposes merciless vengeance, in Jesus' name (1: 6–8), and deliberately whips up further eschatological anxiety in the community with lurid visions directed against he 'who opposes and exalts himself against every so-called god or object of worship, so that he takes his seat in the temple of God, proclaiming himself to be God: (2: 4). In conclusion, he makes his stand upon the truth (ἀλήθεια) against which no argument is possible, since any deviation from it is itself God-given and leads to condemnation. As Paul puts it, 'Therefore God sends upon them a strong delusion, to make them believe what is false' (2: 11). Divine authority – and therefore Paul's – is underlined insofar as it stretches even to control over its own rejection.

II Thessalonians has the effect of engendering an anxiety which makes a community submissive. Its rhetoric well fulfils the definition of the art of rhetoric by Socrates in the *Phaedrus* as 'a method of influencing men's minds by means of words, whether the words are spoken in a court of law or before some other public body or in private conversation'.[15] Graham Shaw in his book *The Cost of Authority* (1983) concludes that Paul's rhetorical exercise of authority in I and II Thessalonians

. . . fosters illusions, it contradicts itself, it demands alienation, and is stubbornly repressive. Already the gospel is understood as a privilege which reflects and reinforces the alienation of a religious élite from others. As persecution and social antagonism increase, it can only take refuge in a growing stress on retribution. It is impossible to reconcile such a belief with any authentic love. The tension of waiting reinforces the anxiety of the believers and their hostility to the outside world, and the preoccupation with the future encourages fantasy.[16]

This altogether bleak and humourless view of Paul's writings has been endorsed by my own present study, and is entirely unrepresented by George Kennedy, who recognises Paul's rhetorical subtlety but without moral or theological comment in his book *New Testament Interpretation Through Rhetorical Criticism*. Nor can I in this chapter do much more than present to you what I see as a profound problem for Pauline studies, if not Christian theology as a whole. For in his early letters Paul appears to be a man beset by self-doubt and insecurity, and using considerable rhetorical skill to manipulate his audience and establish his authority. It is precisely an exercise of that verbal skill which Plato suspects in the *Phaedrus*, and which is to be distinguished, in the celebrated discourse on love in that Dialogue, from wisdom and truth and is entirely lacking the subtle ironic reasonings with which Socrates entraps his own reasoning. Paul's doctrine, it seems, cannot be distinguished from the political and personal motives of his writing, or the uneasiness of his relation to his readers. The assertion of authority and the exercise of personal power are dominant themes of these letters.

However, I readily recognise that my texts are probably the earliest of Paul's epistles. Is it fair to assume that such is the case throughout the whole corpus of his later writings? I have time to offer only one hint that it may not *entirely* be so, though I do not think that, even in the Letter to the Romans, Paul actually develops what Wilhelm Wuellner calls 'the rhetoric of faith argumentation'.[17] It may be the case, however, that he does demonstrate a more developed insight into theological wisdom, and truth and freedom, and precisely by means of an increasingly subtle sense of the inherent ambiguities within the language of power. Thus, Romans 13: 1–10 might be seen as both an exercise of power and a refusal of power. The familiar passage begins, 'Let every person be subject to the governing authorities' (13: 1). Quite literally it seems, the gospel appears to demand of Christians complete submission to secular authority as a matter of conscience. As usual, Paul prefers a docile, submissive community, and on the face of it, Christians are denied the radical newness of life transfigured by obedience to the crucified and risen Lord.

But, by now we should be suspicious of the word 'literal'. As Anders Nygren in his *Commentary on Romans*

(1949) has reminded us, Paul was anxious lest Christians become blindly enthusiastic about their new freedom promised in the 'new aeon' so that they come to regard the order of life in the 'old aeon', which is still with us, with anarchic indifference. Bishop Nygren comments:

> Here Paul takes a most emphatic position against the fanatical view which makes the gospel into a law for society . . . The two aeons do interpenetrate, but that does not mean that they may be arbitrarily confused.[18]

The key word in the passage, it seems to me, appears in verse 8 ('Owe no one anything except to love one another') – the word 'ὀφείλετε' balanced as it is between the two phrases 'one must be subject' (v. 5), and 'except to love one another' (v. 8). The Greek verb has a double sense – 'owe' meaning 'being in debt', or 'owe' meaning 'being obligated'. In this double meaning, as it is exercised in this passage, may be recognised a Pauline rhetoric of irony, a new note not present in the earlier writings, and constituting a reflective in-breaking into the community's self-perception whereby its reconstitution into a church of obedience is radically disturbed in the duality of ὀφείλετε. This new definition becomes, through its rhetorical and persuasive nature, both an exercise of power and also a refusal of power. Applied to the state ὀφείλετε is used in the first sense of 'being in debt'. Applied to the neighbour (ἀλλήλους) it is used in the second sense of 'being obligated'. The Christian should not be indebted to the state, but is obligated to the neighbour, to unrestricted love. Once this radical moment is acknowledged, one is caught in the powerful drive, fuelled by the linguistic tension, between a negative, indifferent obedience and a responsible, energetic 'freedom in the spirit of which Christ's authority under God is already a foretaste'.[19]

I conclude with a brief question. Does the rhetoric of St Paul's letters simply enact a propagation of Pauline authority and apostolic power, or does Paul come to recognise that actually a subversion of that rhetoric from within and by its own tropes, by linguistic ambiguity and irony, represents a proper support of freedom and autonomy within the Christian gospel whereby, in fact, his true apostolic status is recognised and preserved? It is a question which is addressed further in the conclusion of the next chapter, after the rhetoric of St Mark's Gospel has been examined in some detail.

Notes

1. Robert Scholes, *Textual Power* (Yale, 1985) p. 165.
2. Peter Dixon, *Rhetoric*. p. 71.
3. George A. Kennedy, *New Testament Interpretation Through Rhetorical Criticism*. p. 7.
4. See, George A. Kennedy, *Classical Rhetoric and Its Christian and Secular Tradition from Ancient to Modern Times*. pp. 121–5.
5. See, Chaim Perelman, *The Realm of Rhetoric* (Notre Dame, 1982) p. 6.
6. Ibid. p. 20.
7. See, Graham Shaw, *The Cost of Authority* (London, 1983) p. 157.
8. C.F.D. Moule, *The Birth of the New Testament*. 2nd Ed. (London, 1966) p. 210.
9. Chaim Perelman and L. Olbrechts-Tyteca, *The New Rhetoric: A Treatise on Argumentation*. (Notre Dame, 1971) p. 14.
10. Perelman, *The Realm of Rhetoric* p. 125, c.p. also Jacques Derrida, 'White Mythology: Metaphor in the Text of Philosophy'. Trans. F.C.T. Moore, *New Literary History* 6 (1974) 5–74.
11. Walter Ong, *Orality and Literacy* (London and New York, 1982): Wolfgang Iser, *The Implied Reader* (Baltimore and London, 1974): Robert Detweiler (Ed.), *Reader Response Approaches to Biblical and Secular Texts. Semeia* 31 (1985).
12. Walter Wink, *Naming the Powers*. Vol. I of, *The Powers*. (Philadelphia, 1984) p. 130.
13. See passim, Graham Shaw, op. cit. pp. 29–40.
14. See, Perelman, *The Realm of Rhetoric*. p. 95.
15. Plato, *Phaedrus* 261A. Trans., p. 73.
16. Shaw, op. cit. pp. 39–40.
17. Wuellner, 'Paul's Rhetoric of Argumentation in Romans' *Catholic Biblical Quarterly* 38 (1976) 351.
18. Anders Nygren, *Commentary on Romans* (Philadelphia, 1949) p. 426.
19. Paul Lehmann, *The Transfiguration of Politics. Jesus Christ and the Question of Revolution*. (London, 1975) p. 38.

4

The Community of St Mark's Gospel: Let the Reader Understand

The right thing in speaking really is that we should be satisfied not to annoy our hearers, without trying to delight them: we ought in fairness to fight our case with no help beyond the bare facts: nothing, therefore, should matter except the proof of those facts. Still, as has been said, other things affect the result considerably, owing to the defects of our hearers.

Aristotle, *Rhetoric*

It is no bad thing for an author to establish a certain authority of manner, if possible, in the early stages of his writing since, thereby, the gravity of form might carry more easily with it whatever substance may be implied. Certainly there is good precedent for this in the theory and practice of rhetoric. It may, of course, be the case that the assertion of superiority by the suggestion that your readers' understanding is defective is neither amiable nor particularly effective and certainly in the face of either an academic or critical community – but perhaps within our present textual relationship, the reader and I can smile together since I, too, am a member of the reading, literary community, isolated for a moment (as all of us are, from time to time) for praise or blame in order that the community as a whole may sharpen its wits and reassure itself that we may be a community, forged perhaps upon the sense of alienation of each of its members, but a community still.

I have begun this chapter by briefly exploring the given relationship – in rhetorical criticism termed the *aptum*[1] – between the three fundamental terms of an argumentation: the relationship between speaker and speech content, between speaker and audience, and between speech content and audience. I suggest that insofar as the question raised in Chapter 2 (p. 32) of both the interrelation and interdependence of form and content (*res* and *verba*) is here raised, the *aptum* is the crucial hermeneutical issue.[2] The situation is granted further complication by the confusion which we readily recognise, and usually fail to take seriously enough, that what we say and what we mean may be, consciously or unconsciously, two quite different things. As we struggle to clarify the *aptum* of speaker–audience, and the *aptum* of the audience–speech content, the textual situation in which all meet contains within itself a wilful undercurrent of argumentation, recognised perhaps in the structuralist distinction between 'deep structure' and 'surface discourse', in the discovery of paradigmatic patterns embedded in the syntagm of the surface discourse.[3] But let us not assume that this is a twentieth-century discovery, for classical rhetoricians were discussing the same issue as the *intellectio* by the writer concerning the nature of the *quaestio* and the *status* or *stasis*, that is the underlying key-issue, before he carries out or enacts (*actio*) the surface *causa*.[4] The clarification of the *aptum* leads directly to one of the central issues in all rhetorical criticism: that is, the establishment of where, in a given text and its reception, the power is located which generates effects and, perhaps, what we call, with fearless optimism, its meaning. Do we search *within* the terms of its textuality, or rest satisfied that the energy comes from without in referential terms of being and reality? Does the former option imply a pure formalism, without option, and the ultimate death of meaning and sense?

As we come particularly to the texts of the New Testament, where is the locus of power which drives its rhetorical machinery of persuasion? One answer, a familiar and comfortable one (though fraught with its own danger), is suggested by a distinguished New Testament critic with a particular sensitivity to early Christian rhetoric. In the introduction to the 1971 reissue of his formative work, *Early Christian Rhetoric*, Amos Wilder writes:

> What is crucial . . . is that all such manifold particularity in the language and the language events – in the various genres, voices and images – requires a corresponding rich structure in Reality itself, in Being itself.[5]

This 'ultimate mystery', then, is cast outside the text, relieving it of responsibility and defusing the crucial meeting point between the elements of rhetorical interplay – the *aptum* – in a typical escape. But, in the fabric and the compositional structure of early Christian rhetoric, wherein is located the drive to power? One thing seems to be clear, as we have already perceived in the writings of Paul, that the argumentative nature of religious literature demands a methodology that can give an account of the nature and effects of argumentation.[6] As I have already suggested, modern scholars of rhetoric seem to be generally agreed that at the heart of religious rhetoric, quite distinctively, lies in authoritative proclamation and not in rational persuasion.[7] But the consequences of this absolute, rhetorical demand have not been properly recognised. Most radically, and more disturbing even than Paul, such rhetoric is operative within the Gospel of Mark wherein language, it seems, tends towards an absolute claim to truth without evidence and without recourse to logical argument.

The tone is set in the first few verses – assertive, absolute, pitched without compromise. We may compare Jesus' initial proclamation of the gospel in Mark with the version in Matthew. There the call to repentence is delivered in a form which classical rhetoric would term an *enthymeme*.

Μετανοεῖτε · ἤγγικεν γὰρ ἡ βασιλεία τῶν οὐρανῶν.
(Matthew 4: 17)

In the enthymeme a supporting reason is always given. In Mark, however, the gospel is purely proclaimed, not as an enthymeme, but as four authoritative moments: the time is fulfilled, the kingdom of God is at hand, repent, believe in the gospel (Mark 1: 15). Indeed, as Professor Kennedy has noted, the enthymeme is very largely absent from the Gospel of Mark, which stands beside Matthew almost bare of argumentation, its radical rhetoric stark in its assertion of authority and mysterious, threatening, confusing power.

In consequence it is not sufficient, it seems to me, to conclude with Kennedy that 'Mark is seemingly addressed to devout Christians who want a written account of the sayings and deeds of Jesus in simple terms that they can understand and use in the life and worship'.[8] Such claims for simplicity just do not match the rhetorical claims of the Gospel's narrative, which proclaim to us as Frank Kermode so powerfully stated in *The Genesis of Secrecy* (1979) 'that stories can always be enigmatic, and can sometimes be terrible. And Mark's gospel as a whole – to put the matter too simply – is either enigmatic and terrible, or as muddled as the commentators say this passage is (Mark 4: 10–12) . . . Mark is a strong witness to the enigmatic and exclusive character of narrative, to its property of banishing interpreters from its secret places'.[9]

The 'Messianic Secret'; 'say nothing to anyone' (Mark 1: 44); the muddled confusion of the disciples; 'they began to beg Jesus to depart from their neighbourhood' (Mark 5: 17); 'Get behind me, Satan!' (Mark 8: 33); the boy in the linen shirt (Mark 14: 51–2); 'ἐφοβοῦντο γάρ' ('for they were afraid') (Mark 16: 8): are these the simple terms of a gospel proclaimed to be understood and used in every-day life and worship?

According to Eusebius[10] the Gospel of Mark arose out of a request by churches which had been founded by St Peter for a written text of the gospel which they could use after Peter himself had left them and moved on. In other words, this Gospel was conceived as an address to an already established Christian community; to convinced Christians. If this is so, it seems to me to be crucial, for I want to suggest that the rhetorical demands of this text have developed out of a newly-established community wishing to assert its identity and sense of mutual inter-dependence by an act of self-entextualising – asserting the 'content' of its being in the 'form' of a rhetorical construct which both realises and enacts its necessary moment of power and authority.

I suggest further, drawing upon the insights of a remarkable essay by Donald Pease entitled 'Critical Com-munities',[11] that two models may be proposed as illus-trative of the formation of such a coherent group with the necessary internal strength and energy.

a.   The group which derives its cohesion from the power exerted by the threat of alienation of each member of the group. The rhetoric of the defining texts enacts a 'discourse of repression'[12] in which the conditions of alienation are recognised by each individual who, by virtue of the common text, retreats into the false security of a group powerfully bound together by their specific, furtively repressed, anxieties.

b. The group organised by the logic of what Sartre called a 'group-in-formation'. In this model each member acts in a situation of mediation to every other member of the group, his position being 'a context for reflecting on the common project that draws him in relation to the rest of the group'.[13] In this model, although difference becomes the basis for further development, the group project does actually become a means of both defining and developing each individual member. Is this the model in essence adopted by Paul to overcome the near-surrealistic picture of the church in Corinth (I Corinthians 12: 15 ff) as a community withering under the experience of in-dividuals projecting themselves or alternatively feeling excluded through the lack of a powerful cohesive element in the rhetoric of their self-identity?[14]

Let me try to justify my use of this last term as I turn back to the Gospel of Mark, and apply to it my first model of a critical community. In the terms of that model, the anxiety experienced under threat of alienation is produced insofar as the community is actually unwilling to admit any radical discontinuity in its appropriation of the gospel.

To you has been given the secret of the Kingdom of God, but for those outside everything is in parables.
(Mark 4: 11)

For the group within there is no prior moment of destruction (deconstruction?) Instead, a more pervasive, more seductive strategy is assumed in the easier terms of simply opposing the new to the old, a procedure of modernisation.

But the community thus self-constituted is betrayed by its own rhetoric, for the necessary repression required to assert continuity will reveal the threadbare, ragged features of that which lies outside the power structures erected by the huddled community of lonely, frightened individuals. The ragged figure, in the necessary moment of ontological destruction, has not been recognised, the priority of its authority not insisted upon.[15]

Of what, therefore, were they afraid? 'And they were filled with awe (φόβον μέγαν)' (Mark 4: 41); 'and they were afraid' (Mark 5: 15); 'for they all saw him and were terrified' (Mark 6: 50); 'for they were afraid' (Mark 16: 8).

Is it a rhetorical betrayal that lies at the root of this anxiety? In answer to this I adopt a rhetorical vocabulary which has been recently used to brilliant effect by David Klemm in an analysis of tropes in postmodern theological enquiry. Fascinated by this enquiry I began to wonder what would be the result of putting the Gospel of Mark through the same analysis.

Klemm concentrates upon the four master tropes of thought and discourse: metaphor, metonymy, synecdoche and irony,[16] ordered by Giambattista Vico in *The New Science* (1744), and re-established more recently by Kenneth Burke, Hayden White and Paul Ricoeur.[17] The pattern moves from a primary *metaphorical* perspective on reality, to a *metonymic* analysis (described by Kenneth Burke as the *'reduction* of some higher or more complex realm of being to the terms of a lower or less complex realm of being'),[18] to the *synecdochic* reassembly of the elements of metonymic reduction, to an *ironic* dialectic as a reflexive comprehension of synecdochic integration. The last phase, of course, is crucial, in breaking down a false idolatry or rescuing discourse from merely gambolling over the abyss in playful, rhetorical irresponsibility. The pattern is, admittedly, a convention, but arguably rooted deeply in biblical narrative and serving necessarily to remind us that understanding is lodged within our sensitivity to the linguistic practice of mediation between conceptual thinking and prereflective experience.

My contention is that our difficulty with the Gospel of Mark seen in terms of the first model of community, lies in the absence from its rhetorical pattern of the last of the four master tropes – irony. It is that absence of the ironic, of reflective comprehension and an ability to stand outside the rhetorical strategy which flings the community that generated the text back upon itself in a frenzy of repressed anxiety and ultimate refusal to change.

'He would not permit the demons to speak, because they knew him' (Mark 1: 34). The possession of the interpretative key in Mark is demonic, because that immediately affirms a locus of power outside the claims of the entextualised community. The repression of the Messianic Secret, the repressive mystery of the parables (and even those 'inside' apparently fail to grasp the point 'for their hearts were hardened' Mark 6: 52), the blindness of the disciples, the blank fear of the women rushing out of the tomb – all combine to reinforce the authority of a group maintained by the anxiety engendered in each individual through rhetorical strategy. Dare one admit one's alienation from the fundamental relationship – the *aptum* – presupposed in Mark 13: 14, 'ὁ ἀναγινώσκων νοείτω' – 'let the reader understand'? The phrase, of course, can be read in many ways – assuming a secret complicity between reader and author; the genuine ignorance of the author saying 'make of that what you can'. But what does the reader understand? Only that a community is being assumed, and that there is knowledge which he cannot afford not to possess. What manipulation is being contrived here?

Scholars, of course, gleefully establish their own community by proposing answers to the riddle, proposing a background which will grant an origin to the mystery. But the mystery is the Sphinx which is met upon the road back to origins,[19] and the Sphinx is our anxiety. In the Gospel of Mark only the demons hold the interpretative key, while for everyone else there is only hardness of heart, the mystery, the secret of the fear which thrusts us away from the moment in the tomb. On the cross, the cry of dereliction – why not dereliction? But that moment is most powerful to cast us back into the arms of the community and the God from whom in reality we are alienated. There *is* no interpretative key, only blankness, and if it were otherwise the power of the rhetoric would be loosened.

Frank Kermode has suggested that 'Matthew took the first step toward reducing the bleak mystery of Mark's proposals',[20] replacing Mark's 'ἵνα' with 'ὅτι' (Mark 4: 12;

Matthew 13:15). The mystery of parables told in Mark's Gospel apparently to prevent understanding, is reversed by Matthew, so that they are told *because* the people do not understand. Matthew offers a more 'sensible', a more 'sane' reading. Luke, perhaps, goes even further than Matthew in the process of the domestication of the church's authority, adding argumentation and amplification to the bare Marcan rhetoric. Cleopas and his companion in Emmaus recognise the stranger, who had walked with them, in the eucharistic breaking of the bread (Luke 24: 30–1), an interpretative key which opens to them the mystery of their encounter, and a key guarded closely within the comfortable and comforting domesticity of the church's sacraments.

No such domestic structure rationalises the drive to power in the text of the Gospel of Mark. Failing entirely in the moment of irony which establishes the proper distance between God and the symbol of God – a necessary act of literary self-reflection – the Gospel declines to make any distinction between *priority* and *authority*[21] and, emptied of historical content, simply sets the new in opposition to what has become merely obsolescent. The authoritative claim of the Gospel is absolute, the apparent achievement in literary creativity of the ambition of Borges' Pierre Menard who proposed to write, word for word and line for line, *the Quixote itself*:

My intent is no more than astonishing . . . The final term in a theological or metaphysical demonstration – the objective world, God, causality, the forms of the universe – is no less previous and common than my famed novel.[22]

This isolation from what has gone before, not in terms of historical radical discontinuity, but rather of an absolute claim to authority is a form of *kenosis*, an 'undoing' of the precursor's strength in order to isolate the moment of

power repeated in the self.[23] Priority is emptied, so that
we are left amazed and asking, 'What is this? διδαχὴ
καινὴ κατ ἐξουσίαν – (A new teaching! With authority
. . .)' (Mark 1: 27). Here is no Pauline kenosis, but a
daemonic parody of it (one has always known that the
demons held the interpretative key in Mark), humbling
not the self but all precursors in a grand act of ultimate
defiance: in the rhetoric of the Gospel to choose between
the textual community or the admission of fear unto death.
In Harold Bloom's discussion of this moment we are
reminded of Blake's cry to Tirzah:

> Whate'er is Born of Mortal Birth,
> Must be consumed with the Earth
> To rise from Generation free;
> Then what have I to do with thee?[24]

In working thus with my first model of a critical community, the rhetoric of power in the Gospel of Mark, fearful
of irony, leads us to a terrible Nietzschean vision of a
church whose 'conscious misery is set up as the perfection
of the world's history'.[25]

But what now of the second model, the model of Sartre's
'group-in-formation'? As an image of a community
struggling to assert its identity through an exercise in
textuality, does this model illuminate for us more sharply
and properly the terrible majesty of the Gospel of Mark?
Having glanced at the worst, the significant point is to be
made in the crucial absence from the rhetorical pattern of
the Gospel of the moment of irony under the terms of the
first model of the critical community. But is this also true
under the terms of the second model?

I believe it is not, and the significance of this is to be
recognised in an important revision of the article by David
Klemm to which I have already referred.

We need to be reminded of the nature of the second
model.[26] In such a group every member provides a

moment of reflection based upon his difference from the
other members of the group in their common task of
the building of the whole body. The community thus
becomes, in the activity of mutual reflection and self-
reflection, an interdependent organism which also
defines and encourages the task of each individual. It is
engendered and strengthened, therefore, by repeated acts
of reflexive comprehension – in Klemm's terms by the
final figure of *irony*. Furthermore, if, as we have seen, the
first model of community, rhetorically structured upon
the threat of alienation, is unwilling or unable to admit of
any radical discontinuity, this second model of 'group-
in-formation', both tolerates and welcomes the critical
reaction, the moment at which ironic reflection recognises the radical turn, the discontinuity which does not
merely oppose the new to the old, but in a deconstructive
spirit exhilaratingly collapses the dangerous edifices in
the lumber-room of our inheritance. The shock may be
profound, traumatic.

καὶ μετὰ τὸ παραδοθῆναι τὸν Ἰωάννην ἦλθεν ὁ Ἰησοῦς
(Now after John was arrested, Jesus came . . .)' (Mark
1: 4):

'Get behind me, Satan! For you are not on the side of
God, but of men' (Mark 8: 33. I will return to this
passage of Peter's confession at Caesarea Philippi in
more detail later):

'With men it is impossible, but not with God; for all
things are possible with God' (Mark 10: 27).

In rehearsing the fourfold rhetorical pattern of metaphor,
metonymy, synecdoche and irony, Klemm identifies
synecdoche (when elements are reconstituted into a new
figure) as marking the inbreaking of God from outside
the linguistic structure. This moment of summation he

applies to the conventions of biblical narrative and the theologies constructed from it.[27] I want to suggest that this moment of 'inbreaking into the linguistic structure' can only take place in any sense *ironically* and in terms of 'otherness'. And it is 'the element of irony' which is precisely missing from that anxious, repressed model of community which I have hitherto applied to the Gospel of Mark: a community formed by a rhetoric of power which both alienates and dictates – a church outside of which there is no salvation, for there is indeed nothing but the threat of fear and the fear of nothingness.

May we, then, recover the ironic moment of divine reflexivity in the Gospel, a moment which can only be grasped by a community whose defining rhetoric can embrace the shock of radical discontinuity? An essential attribute of God?[28] In his book *A Rhetoric of Irony* (1974), Wayne Booth writes of such that

> In the kind we turn to finally, infinite but somehow stable, the ironist of infinities suggests that there is, after all, a Supreme Ironist, truth itself, standing in his temple above us, observing all authors and readers in their comic or pathetic or tragic efforts to climb and join him. For such an ironist it is not so much the whole of existence that is absurd as it is mankind in the proud claim to know something about it. His works may in some respects resemble Beckett's: every proposition will be doubted as soon as uttered, then undercut by some other proposition that in turn will prove inadequate. The meanings are finally covert. But both the effort to understand and the particular approximations, inadequate as they are, will be worthwhile; the values are stable.
>
> The picture of God or Truth as supreme ironist, incomprehensible and infinitely distant, may superficially resemble the picture of an impersonal universe that indifferently (and hence brutally) frustrates all

human effort at statement. But the form of 'reading assignment' given by the two views is radically different. For the second, infinite ironies present finally a treadmill, each step exactly like every other, the final revelation always the same: *nada*. Since the universe is empty, life is empty of meaning, and every reading experience can finally be shaken out into the same empty and melancholy non-truth. But for the first, the universe, though deceptive, is infinitely, invitingly various; each flash or ironic insight can lead us toward others, in a game never ending but always meaningful and exhilarating.[29]

It is upon this 'reading assignment' that we are now embarked, and in due course I will have occasion to offer a radical criticism of Professor Booth's position. Nevertheless, the idea of God as ironist is by no means absent from literature (see below Chapter 9), and ours is not the dark road of melancholy non-truth, but a path which is, I believe, meaningful and can be exhilarating.

Consider the cry of the soldiers in the Gospel of Mark, uttered in derision of the Lord in bondage:

> And they clothed him in a purple cloak, and plaiting a crown of thorns they put it on him. And they began to salute him, 'Hail, King of the Jews!' And they struck his head with a reed, and spat upon him, and they knelt down in homage to him.
>
> (Mark 15: 17–19)

In the context of the Gospel, as Wayne Booth has pointed out,[30] there is a double irony; the irony of the soldiers railing against their victim, and the irony of the Gospel against the original ironists. And it is this second 'literary' irony which recognises the fundamental textual strategy which cuts through the instabilities of interpretation and military game-playing: that the forlorn,

unlikely figure is, in fact, the King of the Jews. Furthermore, this generation of ironic pathos effects a binding
together of the community of those who are brought to
perceive the essential, pathetic power of the situation in
the context established by the text.

The strength of the irony depends upon the radical
rhetoric of Mark. In the Fourth Gospel, elaboration weakens the irony and changes the whole point:

> Pilate also wrote a title and put it on the cross; it read,
> 'Jesus of Nazareth, the King of the Jews'. Many of the
> Jews read this title, for the place where Jesus was cru-
> cified was near the city; and it was written in Hebrew,
> in Latin, and in Greek. The chief priests of the Jews
> then said to Pilate 'Do not write, "The King of the
> Jews", but, "This man said, I am King of the Jews"'.
> Pilate answered, 'What I have written I have written'.
> (John 19: 19–22).[31]

Finally, Booth has noted, the community of readers united
by its grasp of this radical irony in Mark, is larger and
with fewer outsiders, than any that could be built upon a
literal statement of beliefs. Such ironic form binds by its
pathos and its generation of sympathy – a sympathy
which is humanly felt even in the unbeliever who would
retreat from any straightforward affirmation that Jesus
was the King of the Jews, the Messiah, the Son of God.

And so, by this rhetorical device we have relocated the
moment of power, not in the drive of the community to
exert its influence by the threat of alienation, but in a
doubly ironic demand, a reflexive rhetoric which defuses
the power politics of community and its intersubjective
relations; a demand which draws forth sympathy and
prompts self-reflection and reflection upon the common
situation through the position of a mediatory figure, in
the ironic, dialectical relation of negation and affirmation.
It is upon this ironic moment, therefore, that our second

model of community – a community realised as
entextualised in the provision of the Gospel – that, if
anywhere, God's inbreaking is remarked as a trace, an
absolute otherness, upon the linguistic structure.
And the inbreaking and subsequent persuasive
entextualisation recognise a radical discontinuity in the
formation of the group. Was this the Messiah of our
hopes? This figure who engenders fear and perplexity,
who hangs on the gibbet, a thing accursed? The experience
seen as text is well described (I am not sure if there is not
irony here!) by Harold Bloom: 'most so-called "accurate"
interpretations of poetry are worse than mistakes; perhaps
there are only more or less creative or interesting misreadings'.[32] The authority claimed within the ironic rhetorical moment admits, in one sense, a formal lack of
distinction between priority and authority. In this it seems
to be one within the pattern of the first model of community through which I approached the Gospel of Mark.
What has gone before is abandoned in the creative mis-
reading, the 'σκάνδαλον' of the text. But it is a misread-
ing, not an abandonment, a radical newness which does
not derive its absolute claims upon us purely from within
the conscious misery of its own rhetorical and textual
perfection. It is a *kenosis* which is not simply an 'undoing'
of prior strength in order to isolate the moment of power
repeated in the self. Rather, it is a kenosis which is utterly
radical, daring a uniqueness which no other creative act
of poetry or making, could bear – for in poets mis-reading
is an act of aggression whereby predecessors in the art
are undone in a false display of individual talent and self-
aggrandisement. But in the greatest of all ironies, and
within the self-satisfaction of rhetoric, the mis-reading is
found to be the true reading, a persuasive act achieved
only by a self-emptying, an utterly powerful isolation on
a turning point – the tree – when the past and the present
are transfigured in the one true moment of poetry which
achieves what all poetry aspires to, a timelessness which

history cannot tolerate, but which changes history. In that moment of irony, the *aptum* is, for once, not a matter for rhetorical criticism to discuss, but remains rhetorically beyond rhetoric in recognition and contemplation. In any other poet or text, it would be the moment of death in a supreme isolation and solipsism.

> Do nothing from selfishness or conceit, but in humility count others better than yourselves. Let each of you look not only to his own interests, but also to the interests of others. Have this mind among yourselves, which is yours in Christ Jesus, who, though he was in the form of God, did not count equality with God a thing to be grasped, but emptied himself, taking the form of a servant, being born in the likeness of men. And being found in human form he humbled himself and became obedient unto death, even death on a cross.
>
> (Philippians 2: 3–8)

In conclusion, I want to suggest that this latter reading of the radical Christian rhetoric of the Gospel of Mark requires us to recognise an early Christian community which was formed upon dynamics which are the same as those described by St Paul in I Corinthians 12 in terms of the *body of Christ*. At this stage, therefore, I want to continue to expand a little my discussion of Paul's writings in the previous chapter. The Marcan community required its written gospel, perhaps in the first instance to compensate for the absence of St Peter, but more fundamentally because it required a text whose rhetoric would define it under the particular persuasion of an authority, recognised and exercised rhetorically.

The metaphor used by Paul of, in Günther Bornkamm's terms, 'a unified yet many-membered organism in which each member has its function and the whole could not remain alive without each'[33] was a common one in the ancient world, and bears a remarkable similarity to our image of a community as 'group-in-formation'. As each individual in his or her uniqueness becomes a context for the necessary reflection upon the common project, so the group is not bound by the threat of alienation, but by a vital adhesion to a common task of mutual regard which both defines and ensures the well-being of the whole. For, 'if one member suffers, all suffer together; if one member is honoured, all rejoice together' (I Corinthians 12: 26).

Furthermore, such a community can only continue to exist under the central, formative drive of an ambivalent, ironic affirmation, which is also a denial, and can only be sustained in terms of a unique fulcrum of power with which each individual identifies, and yet which stands entirely isolated, a means of corporate identity; a crisis of authority which is also a promise of freedom. David Klemm describes the figure of this ironic affirmation:

> . . . the figure of Jesus presents not only the meaning of authentic human being in faith but also the being of God. How so? The symbol not only presents me with the 'I' of faith as my own otherness but also discloses what it means for God to be God – namely not to be aloof, impersonal deity but to be approaching each I with its own otherness.[34] Jesus, symbol of authentic faith, is symbol of God only through the cross of Christ – through Jesus' own denial that Jesus is God.[35] The symbol of God denies that it literally is God and thus affirms itself as *symbol* of God . . . Jesus denies that he is God and yet performs the being of God.[36]

In the rhetoric of irony the dead-letter of literalism[37] is enlivened by the literary which affirms an authentic faith. Power is asserted as freedom only in bondage, and the premature immediate celebration of the messianic presence is in fact demonic, requiring, like the demons in the Gospel of Mark who readily recognise Jesus, a

peremptory command to silence. Or, more dramatically
in the Gospel, Peter's too ready rebuke of Jesus' predic-
tion of the sufferings of the Son of Man (Mark 8: 31–3) is
immediately recognised as a Satanic failure to understand the ambiguity of the presence of power in the world
of human affairs; that it requires a revolutionary subversion involving a denial and a 'verbal' affirmation, not of
God, but of what it means for God to be God. The irony
draws the necessary gap between the symbol of God and
God, for it is the power of the symbol (the broken figure
hailed, ironically, as King of the Jews) to confirm that
which can never literally be seen or grasped – and if it
were it would not in any sense be true. Drawn by its
pathos, which Peter wanted to deny, we come to affirm,
in Booth's words, 'the immense sureties of interpretation
that can be given an ironic passage by a fully developed
literary context like that provided by Mark'.[38] But I do not
wish to be misunderstood. For my sense of what Booth
calls 'sureties' lies in notions of liberation, deconstructive
freedom and the affirmative suffering of those who do
not wish to foreclose thought.

It is precisely this affirming, hermeneutical dialectic,
perceived most radically in the Gospel of Mark, which
allows us to perceive at work in the Pauline community
of the later letters a 'transfiguration of politics', to use
Paul Lehmann's term,[39] which is brought about by a
Christian rhetoric, a rhetoric transformed by a radical
shift of power and therefore a shift in the fundamental
terms of argumentation.

It was in this spirit that I reconsidered Romans 13: 1–10
as an exercise of power and a refusal of power (see above
pp. 46–7). By this the Pauline church is continually stirred
into radical reflection by that tension and energy which
necessitates and engenders its rhetoric, its entextualising.

One of the most stimulating, perceptive and provoking
studies of the Gospel of Mark in recent years is Dan Via's
The Ethics of Mark's Gospel – In the Middle of Time (1985).

I refer to it finally because Professor Via is a New Testament critic who is deeply appreciative of the ways of literature and sensitive to the proper and necessary integration of the manifold concerns of interpretation, in this instance literary criticism, biblical studies and constructive theological ethics. But I refer to it also because it seems to me that in his conclusion Via collapses the rhetorical dimension of this Gospel in favour of a critical systematic attempt to rationalise and conclude. He refers to William Wrede's long-established presentation of Jesus as both the revealed and concealed Messiah:

> What Wrede calls contradiction I would call paradox: a logical tension that is yet believed to be necessary to account for reality as experienced. The phenomenon under discussion expresses itself in Mark as two related paradoxes. Revelation when given is still concealed: the disciple stands both before and after resurrection. When revelation does occur, human beings resist the existential entailments of what they know intellectually. These two paradoxes are intertwined in Mark: the full existential appropriation of what is known intellectually is prevented by the incompleteness of the revelation.
>
> The revealed/concealed motif is illuminated by our immediate text (Mark 10: 32–52) and has a bearing on the problem of Mark's use of the narrative form. That Jesus is revealed is seen in the facts that James and John know that he will enter into glory and Bartimaeus senses in him a wonder-working power which he then demonstrates. His true glory is concealed, however, in that it lies within and on the other side of suffering and death (10: 33–4). The concealment is manifested in that James and John do not understand what Jesus' particular kind of glory entails for them (10: 42–4), as is seen in their inappropriate request (10: 36–7). Yet the disciples can at least understand intellectually what Jesus says

about his coming fate, and they must have had some
inkling of its implications for them. Otherwise why
would they be afraid (10: 32)?[40]

This attempt to understand revelation as revealed/con-
cealed, even within Via's discussion of its narrative mode,
seems to me to be ultimately misconceived. For, if approaching the New Testament through the terms and
tropes of classical rhetoric is, as Professor Kennedy
claims,[41] justified both historically and philosophically,
then my enquiry in this chapter has, I hope, indicated the
radical development of such rhetoric in the self-defining
documents of the early Christian Church. Via's 'paradox'
must be further extrapolated from the single moment of
a riddling motif to the drama of a dialectical encounter
enacted only in the pattern of a revolutionary, ironic
rhetoric. Here Kennedy is quite wrong when he argues
that 'Matthew and Paul make extensive use of the *forms*
of logical argument, but the *validity* of their arguments is
entirely dependent on their assumptions, which cannot
be logically and objectively proved'.[42] Rather, the validity
of the arguments of Matthew, Paul, and above all Mark,
is dependent upon a literary necessity which denies the
assumption that validation is granted to textual authority
by the presence/absence, revelation/concealment of God,
in its affirmation of the symbol, or, dare I say, the trace of
an elusive, deferred deity – a synecdoche comprehended
and made powerful by irony.

On the one hand this may be a path to the sad, dis-
appointed agnosticism which awaits the brilliant insights
of Frank Kermode in *The Genesis of Secrecy*, and 'hot for
secrets, our only conversation may be with guardians
who know less and see less than we can; and our sole
hope and pleasure is in the perception of a momentary
radiance, before the door of disappointment is finally
shut on us'.[43] Or, on the other, can a second naïveté[44]
rescue religious experience and the experience of the

church in formation through an indirect, reflective, reflexive, creative adoption of a rhetorical consciousness
which is deeply aware that in text we acknowledge our
metaphorical perspectives, our fictions and our interpretations. To conclude with the nicely-turned exhortation
of Wilhelm Wuellner:

> ... since we are surrounded by a cloud of witnesses of
> rhetoricians, linguistic analysts, structuralists, and oth-
> ers, let us lay aside every weight imposed by priorities
> of traditional historical and literary criticism, and by
> logical and dogmatic preoccupations which cling so
> closely, and let us run with perseverance the race that
> is set before us, looking to Paul [and the Gospel of
> Mark], the pioneers and perfectors of the spirit of faith
> – the rhetoric of faith argumentation.[45]

Yet I am not sure that I would wish to attribute quite so
much even to the later Pauline writings. For if there is to
be a rhetoric of faith it works by subtler and more subversive means than a claim to argumentation, by, indeed,
the dangerous paths of its own tropes in a truly radical
turn of reflexivity.

Notes

1. See, Heinrich Lausberg, *Handbuch der literarischen Rhetorik.*
   (Munich, 1960) Vol. II pp. 54 ff and p. 258.
2. See ibid. Vol. I p. 45 and II pp. 1055–62. Also, Wilhelm Wuellner,
   'Paul's Rhetoric of Argumentation in Romans'. p. 342.
3. See Robert Detweiler, 'After the New Criticism: contemporary
   methods of literary interpretation'. In, Richard A. Spencer (Ed.)
   Orientation by Disorientation (Pittsburgh, 1980) pp. 9–10.
4. See, Wuellner, op. cit. p. 333.
5. Amos Wilder, *Early Christian Rhetoric* (Harvard, 1971) p. xxx.
6. See, Wuellner, op. cit. p. 350. Also Dieter Georgi, 'Forms of Religious Propaganda'. In, H.J. Schultz (Ed.) *Jesus in His Time*
   (Philadelphia, 1971) pp. 124–31.
7. See above Chapter 3, pp. 40–1.

8. Ibid. p. 98.
9. Frank Kermode, *The Genesis of Secrecy* (Harvard, 1979) pp. 33–4.
10. Eusebius, *Church History* 2: 15. See, Kennedy, *New Testament Interpretation Through Rhetorical Criticism* p. 104.
11. In, Joseph A. Buttigeig (Ed.) *Criticism without Boundaries* (Notre Dame, 1987) pp. 92–110.
12. Pease, op. cit. p. 95.
13. Ibid. p. 101.
14. See also, Günther Bornkamm, *Paul*. Trans. D.M.G. Stalker (London, 1969) p. 195.
15. See Harold Bloom, *The Anxiety of Influence* (New York, 1973) pp. 9–10.
16. Klemm, 'Toward a Rhetoric of Postmodern Theology: Through Barth and Heidegger'. pp. 446–7.
17. Kenneth Burke, *Grammar of Motives* (Berkeley and Los Angeles, 1947); Hayden White, *Tropics of Discourse* (Baltimore, 1978); Paul Ricoeur, *Time and Narrative* Vol. III. Trans. Kathleen Blamey and David Pellauer. (Chicago, 1988).
18. Burke, op. cit. p. 506.
19. See, Bloom, op. cit. pp. 36 ff., on the Sphinx and the Covering Cherub.
20. Kermode, op. cit. p. 33.
21. See, Bloom, op. cit. p. 9.
22. Jorge Luis Borges, 'Pierre Menard, Author of the *Quixote*'. In *Labyrinths*. Ed. Donald A. Yates and James E. Irby (Harmondsworth, 1981) p. 66.
23. See, Bloom, op. cit. pp. 87–92.
24. Ibid. p. 92.
25. Nietzsche, quoted in Bloom, op. cit. p. 55.
26. See Pease op. cit. p. 101. Pease in his essay is writing of a critical community of scholars. I am suggesting that the development of the early church, or churches, as communities wrought upon textual definition (in the necessary creation of the gospels, Acts, the epistles, Revelation), should be perceived in terms of a basically similar model.
27. Klemm, op. cit. p. 447.
28. We are properly reminded by Wayne Booth that if, before the eighteenth century, irony was one rhetorical device among many, by the end of the Romantic period it had become something more like the grand Hegelian concept which, it might be said, underlies my present discussion. That may be so. But the Gospel of Mark remains one of the great ironic visions in literature. See, Booth, *A Rhetoric of Irony* (Chicago and London, 1974) p. ix.
29. Ibid. pp. 268–9.
30. Ibid. pp. 28–9, 91–2.
31. Booth points out that further elaboration of the episode in the Mystery Cycles weakens the irony yet more. Ibid. p. 28.
32. Bloom, op. cit. p. 43.

33. Bornkamm, op. cit. p. 194.
34. See also, Robert P. Scharlemann, *The Being of God: Theology and the Experience of Truth.* (New York, 1981) pp. 134–41.
35. See also, Paul Tillich, *Systematic Theology.* Vol. II. Existence and the Christ. (Chicago, 1957) pp. 123–5.
36. Klemm, op. cit. p. 464.
37. See, S.T. Coleridge, *The Statesman's Manual* (1816). 'A hunger-bitten and idea-less philosophy naturally produces a starveling and comfortless religion. It is among the miseries of the present age that it recognises no medium between *Literal* and *Metaphorical.* Faith is either to be buried in the dead letter, or its name and honors usurped by a counterfeit product of the mechanical understanding'. Reprinted in *Lay Sermons. Collected Coleridge* Vol. 6. Ed. R.J. White (Princeton, 1972) p. 30.
38. Booth, *A Rhetoric of Irony.* p. 92.
39. See, Paul Lehmann, *The Transfiguration of Politics* (London, 1975). See also, Chapter 3, note 18.
40. Dan O. Via, Jr. *The Ethics of Mark's Gospel – In the Middle of Time* (Philadelphia, 1985) pp. 172–3.
41. Kennedy, op. cit. p. 10.
42. Ibid. pp. 17–18.
43. Kermode, op. cit. p. 145.
44. The phrase, of course, is Paul Ricoeur's in *The Symbolism of Evil* (1967).
45. Wuellner, op. cit. p. 351. See also above Chapter 3, pp. 39–40.

5

What's a Nice Text Like You Doing in a Place Like This? Archbishop Cranmer's Prayer Book of 1549

If it is true that the community has everything to fear from the sacred, it is equally true that the community owes its very existence to the sacred. For in perceiving itself as uniquely situated outside the sphere of the sacred, the community assumes that it has been engendered by it; the act of generative violence that created the community is attributed not to men, but to the sacred itself. Having brought the community into existence, the sacred brings about its own expulsion and withdraws from the scene, thereby releasing the community from its direct contact.

The more men reflect on the apparent supremacy of the sacred, on the vast disproportion between it and the community, the clearer it becomes that the initiative in all domains, on all levels, belongs to the sacred.[1]

In the light of these remarks, I wish to consider the first wholly vernacular English communion service, that entitled 'The Supper of the Lord and the Holy Communion commonly called the Masse' contained in the *First Prayer Book of Edward VI* (1549). My reason for this is to explore the largely neglected yet crucial role of rhetoric in the liturgy or common worship of a community, and, in the case of the text of 1549, to examine a powerful and cohesive structure in the maintenance of the community which for the first time in the English church, was in a language which all people could understand in its entirety and in which they could participate. Its compulsion, therefore, was all the stronger.

Rhetoric needs to reflect continually on its audience and what it wants its audience to think.[2] Rhetorical writing may be defined quite specifically within the technicalities of the textbooks of rhetoric, or very broadly indeed as a '"deep" human rhetoric, universal to mankind, defined by man's abilities to make certain sounds, symbols and motions and by the nature of his brain'.[3] It is this second definition which more concerns me here, although it is important to recognise that Archbishop Cranmer, the architect of the 1549 Prayer Book, was thoroughly familiar with the techniques of classical and renaissance rhetoric and possessed in his library, for example, Aristotle's *Rhetoric*, Cicero's *De Inventione* and Erasmus' *De Conscribendis*, all crucial technical works.[4]

Chaim Perelman, in his book *The Realm of Rhetoric* (1982), attributes the decline of the art of rhetoric since the end of the sixteenth century to the rise of European bourgeois thought and the emphasis increasingly given to 'evidence'.[5] Argumentation, however, as Aristotle perceived, intervenes where self-evidence is contested and definition is disputed. But equally, where opinions differ, the *process* of argumentation may be powerful to create a particular disposition and claim validity even although its truth cannot *necessarily* and evidentially be established. In Perelman's words, 'the aim of argumentation is not to deduce consequences from given premises; it is rather to elicit or increase the adherence of the members of an audience to theses that are presented for their consent'.[6] Such an audience, society or community adheres to that which ensures their formation and continued identity in 'faith', which in the Greek 'πίστις' is defined by Liddell and Scott as both 'trust in others . . . generally persuasion of a thing' and 'that which gives confidence (or) . . . means of persuasion'.[7] The argument is from authority rather than from demonstrable truth, and controversy does not concern the *argument* itself, but the authority which presents it. The criteria which ultimately establish authority within a community are many – its 'competence', tradition, antiquity, universality[8] – and occasionally its claims may be absolute, justifying, for example, submission to the words of Jesus. In the words of Jacques-Bénigne Bossuet,

> A master (Jesus) who enjoys such great authority, even though his doctrine may be obscure, deserves to have his words believed, *ipsum audite* . . . Do not let us search for the reasons for the truths he teaches us: the whole reason is that he has spoken.[9]

What, then, of the Church which assumes Jesus' 'full authority' (Matthew 28: 18)? The priestly argument from authority – *argumentum ad vericundiam* – based on tradition and scripture, may constitute an immensely powerful instrument of communal control claiming the infallibility of dominical descent, a claim founded upon 'truth', which nevertheless may in the actual terms of its rhetoric, be no more than a deception and the promotion of an abstract truth upheld within a carefully preserved myth. This would be to perceive the Church, following Nietzsche's vision, in the terms of Jacques Derrida's 'White Mythology'.[10]

'Truth' in that case no longer matters. The rhetoric which persuades and preserves the community, once its social order is established, is not necessarily the benign, humane factor which Cicero, for example, in the classical civic tradition, identifies in *De Inventione* as that which 'renders life safe, honourable', protects friends and raises men above the beasts.[11] In the light of this precarious picture, what may be concluded of Archbishop Thomas Cranmer's purpose and achievement in the production of the English Prayer Book of 1549?

Henry VIII died in 1547 and was succeeded on the throne by the youthful Edward VI. From the first it was clear that the reform of worship in the English Reformation Church was to be guided and imposed by political means. Above all the 1549 Act of Uniformity demanded the exclusive use of the liturgy of the new English Prayer Book under threat of severe punishment for those who disobeyed. Sacred authority joined hands with secular in the imposition of the community text. At the heart of it all is the celebration of the communion service and the establishment in the country of 'a uniform, quiet and godly order'.[12] In this task Cranmer was, almost inevitably and despite an increasingly liturgical use of the vernacular, nevertheless bound to the traditional medieval text of the Sarum rite, displaying in his translations from the Latin a style which is characterised by clarity and a desire for structural simplicity. Cranmer further emphasised the didactic need for instruction. He was not, however, simply bound to Sarum, and particularly influential on the communion service was the *Simple and Religious Consultation* of 1545, drawn up by Martin Bucer and Philip Melanchthon for Archbishop Hermann von Wied of Cologne.[13] What is clear is that the service is the conclusion of a long process in Cranmer's work towards a communion service entirely in English, and, as a combination of the medieval rite with changes similar to earlier continental Lutheran reforms and Hermann's *Consultation*,[14] 1549 embraced a broad range of theological opinion while defining a form of worship which would literally be imposed by law and by its own textual authority upon the whole community.

In a letter written at the end of his life to Queen Mary, while awaiting death at her hands, Cranmer justified his liturgy, citing early Christian practice, the command of the Emperor Justinian, but, above all the apostolic authority of St Paul. The Pope himself, Cranmer claimed, in attempting to reimpose the Latin mass on the English people was subverting 'the laws of God':

> . . . God's will and commandment is, that when the people be gathered together ministers should use such language as the people may understand and take profit thereby, or else hold their peace . . . so is it vain and profiteth nothing, saith Almighty God by St. Paul, if the priest speak to the people in a language which they know not . . . that whether the priests rehearse the wonderful works of God, or the great benefits of God unto mankind above all other creatures, or give thanks unto God, or make open confession of their faith, or humble confession of their sins, with earnest request of mercy and forgiveness, or make suit unto God for anything; then all the people, understanding what the priests say, might give their minds and voices with them, and say Amen . . . [15]

Here is a powerful example of the priestly argument from authority – the supreme authority of God by his apostle – controlling the community of the church by a language which, precisely because ordinary folk can understand it, can claim their assent ('Amen') and agreement to whatever the priests may present of the nature of their controlling relationship with God: in the emphasising of his beneficent power, in the confession of faith, in the plea for forgiveness and request for mercy. And so the people become submissive by means of language which, because they understand and trust its familiarity, exercises a powerful art of persuasion upon them.

In such an environment, Christian rhetoric may flourish in what Professor Kennedy describes as 'its purest and most fundamental form', in which the 'basic modes of proof' are 'grace, authority and logos, the divine message which can be understood by man'.[16] In the avoidance of logical argument, however, much may be justified in these terms. In the seventeenth-century treatise *The Art of Speaking* by Bernard Lamy (1675, translated from the French, 1676), we find in the Christian grand style of the Renaissance that 'those who profess Divinity, and would instruct others, must as much as in them lies imitate their great master Christ Jesus, who convinc'd the understanding, wrought upon the will, and inflam'd the heart of his Disciples whilst he taught them'.[17] In the human exercise of power such language is threatening, even and especially when claiming the support of a divine original. It embodies the 'impassionating divine word from the heart of the preacher to the heart of his audience',[18] seeking not to persuade by reason but to signify the control of nothing less than supernatural reality. In the liturgies of the Reformation, the tradition of rhetoric is a basis for the employment of a reformed theology with its antithesis of law and grace, its emphasis on human unworthiness, on faith and the Holy Spirit, which stresses an emotional power operative upon the audience or congregation. In the 1549 service, for example, the moment of the communion is prepared for by the insistent threat of divine 'wrath and indignation' or the promise of God's gracious mercy in the face of our own utter unworthiness. The congregation is gripped by a sense of its own sinfulness, entirely submissive to the power of the sacred rhetoric. Such rhetoric should be seen, therefore, not only as a discipline linking man with God, but more darkly as an instrument of mass persuasion and control.[19]

At this point we seem to be returning, disturbingly, to the world of René Girard's *Violence and the Sacred* with which I began this chapter. Girard uses the image of a ship to describe the community.[20] The ship lives in a dangerous and wilful environment, the ocean, which is both benign and harsh. Only a constant repetition of rites appears to keep the community afloat. But the very rites of the community seem to be the realisation of the supremacy of the sacred which has withdrawn from the scene and yet to which the community owes its very existence. Metaphors of severance permeate the generative act. In the 1549 communion service the congregation make their confession, recognising their severance from God and praying for reconciliation. The so-called 'comfortable words' imply that we are turned away from God. To live with the divine wrath is not possible, yet to live without divine love is impossible. In Girard's words, 'a total separation of the community and the sacred would be fully as dangerous as a fusion of the two'.[21] The religious community, therefore, is bound upon the wheel of a sacred rhetoric whose power is either a deception or an absolute truth – the rhetoric allows no distinction to be made.

What, then, was Cranmer's purpose and intention in 1549? History may, perhaps, provide some answers to that question. But the text of the Prayer Book may be playing other games in its 'deep structure'. Like all texts, 'it is detached from the author at birth [another separation] and goes about the world beyond his power to intend about it or control it'.[22]

It is clear from his work that Thomas Cranmer had learnt well the techniques of rhetoric which made up one-third of the foundation course for undergraduates at the Cambridge of his day. From surviving school notebooks we know that his monarch, Edward VI, was carefully tutored in the standard Latin textbook on rhetoric, *Ad Herrenium*, and knew his Cicero well.[23] Such an education was not unusual, and writing of the Tudor schoolboy, C.S. Lewis perhaps a little donnishly comments that 'you adored sweet Tully (Cicero) and were as concerned about *asyndeton* and *chiasmus* as a modern schoolboy is about cricketers or types of aeroplane'.[24] It is all the more strange, therefore, that Cranmer's work on the Prayer Book has been subjected to no satisfactory analysis of its language from a rhetorical point of view.[25] Even more,

scholars who have subjected the text to rhetorical scrutiny have generally failed to examine the implications of
rhetoric and its techniques for a powerful liturgical text.
C. Watson's study *The Literary Qualities of the Prayer Book*
(1948) may be dismissed simply on the grounds of its
gross inaccuracies. Dr Geoffrey Cumming mentions
rhetoric occasionally in his numerous writings on
Cranmer's work. Professor David Frost, in a brief essay
entitled 'Liturgical Language: Cranmer to Series 3'[26] simply
draws attention to some of the rhetorical devices which
Cranmer employed – antithesis, anaphora, auxesis,
chiasmus, isocolon, and so on. Above all, Cranmer's
constant practice of doubling words and balancing phrases
acts both to fix the language in the mind, while at the
same time to stretch and underline the force of the words,
creating a charged environment for reception and belief.
The phrase 'not waying our merites, but pardoning our
offences', serves to draw us, on the one hand, towards
our own offensive nature while at the same time emphasising not God's condemnation but his pardon. Or
again, on the nature of our sinfulness in the Confession,
we admit that 'the remembrance of them is grievous unto
us, the burthen of them is intollerable'. These balanced
phrases develop an emphasis, from that which is re-
membered to that which is a burden, from that which is
grievous unto us to that which is, in one heavy, stressed
word, 'intollerable'.

Professor Frost quite properly draws attention to such
devices of language, without exploring their effects upon
the community of the church. In this respect, the most
important essay on Cranmer's rhetoric (though dealing
specifically with the Prayer Book of 1552) is by Peter
Mack in the volume edited by myself and R.C.D. Jasper
entitled *Language and the Worship of the Church* (1989). Mack
suggests that we should be careful not to over-emphasise
the role of rhetoric, in the narrow, technical sense in
Cranmer's liturgy. Certainly, engagement with the

liturgy cannot be understood as precisely an experience of argumentation designed to persuade. The rhetoric may, perhaps, be better described as epideictic, that is concerned with praise or blame, with celebration or exhortation.[27] Its effect may be none the less powerful. For example, the first exhortation before Holy Communion in the 1549 service is structured as an oration with a clear narrative development of rhetorically persuasive material which is classical in its form.[28] The introduction establishes the basic premise of the argument, underwritten by the authority of St Paul himself – that the sacrament received with 'a truly penitent heart, and lively fayth' is greatly beneficial, yet received unworthily is a great danger.

The second section of the exhortation enlarges upon the danger to the congregation of unworthy reception of the sacrament. The tone is forceful:

Therfore yf any here bee a blasphemer, aduouterer, or bee in malice, or enuie or in any other greuous cryme . . . lette hym bewaule his synnes, and not come to that holy table, lest after the takyng of that most blessed breade: the devill enter into hym, as he dyd into Iudas, to fyll hym full of all iniquitie, and brynge hym to destruccion, bothe of body and soule.[29]

Those in a state of sin, therefore, are urged to withdraw from the central act which both constitutes and defines the community. The third section, accordingly, offers a bridge, a way out by means of which those in danger of sin are able to judge themselves ('Iudge therfore your selfes (brethen) that ye bee not iudged of the lorde'), and ensure worthy participation in the Communion. The fourth section identifies the act of communicating as a remembrance of Christ, a gift from him and 'a pledge of his love'. The fundamental importance and authority of the Holy Communion is finally thereby underlined, and the whole exhortation is a powerfully persuasive narrative to strengthen the community by stressing individual responsibility, the dire consequences of inappropriate behaviour, and the underlying scriptual and divine authority which claims obedience.

Dare one, or can one contradict such persuasive power? It is felt also in the pithier brevity of many of Cranmer's collects. Perhaps, above all the power of language and its structures to control a submissive audience or congregation is experienced in the 1549 General Confession for Holy Communion, which is based closely on Hermann's *Consultation*.[30] Cranmer's highly Latinate language builds long and weighty grammatical sequences out of short, self-contained units which continually repeat earlier verbal and syntactic patterns. The result is a strong, cohesive whole within which is sustained a repeated bombardment emphasising our weak and sinful natures standing in need of mercy and forgiveness. All is uttered following the initial establishment of the supremacy of God, 'maker of all thinges, iudge of all menne'. The acknowledgement of sin centres upon three rhythmically balanced phrases:

i. our mānifold sīnnes and wȳckedness . . .
ii. thy wrāth and indignācion agāinste us . . .
iii. the būrthen of thēm is intōllerable . . .

These three-stressed phrases move from our sin, to the threat of God's wrath, to the conclusive, heavy syllables of that final, hopeless 'intollerable'. At that point and at that point only is exclaimed the repeated 'have mercie upon us, have mercie upon us, moste mercifull father'.

This concussive series of short, emphatic phrases, building a narrative of confession, is highly effective in transforming a theology into the cry of a community which becomes, by its very language, co-ordinated within particular demands and bound by a fear of the least deviation from them. My concern here is not to engage in a technical discussion of systems of accentual prose rhythm in early English liturgy – whether, for example, Cranmer deliberately used the so-called *cursus*, a rhythmical flow of accents at the end of a phrase or sentence, replacing a different classical system of accentuation employed by Quintilian and other classical rhetoricians.[31] What is important to realise, however, is that prose rhythm is an important and neglected feature of 1549, and that Cranmer is drawing not so much upon a Jewish tradition of worship and liturgy as upon a tradition of classical rhetoric, that is a pagan technique of persuasion which is often associated, primarily through Plato as we have seen, with deception and manipulation beyond the promptings of reason. In the hands of such techniques, theology may begin to play dark games indeed. The possibilities begin to seem highly alarming.

At its best, the situation has been summed up by Debora Shuger in her book *Sacred Rhetoric* (1988), when she writes that:

For the renaissance . . . questions of faith and rhetoric are nearly allied. Faith rests on the unseen, on a promise, whose truth seems contradicted by the empirical evidence. That is, faith, like rhetoric, struggles in the tension between ordinary and spiritual perception, and this struggle to make the invisible and remote subjects of faith luminous and actual relates these issues of seeing and believing to the ancient dilemma and the inverse proportion between *praesentia* and *magnitudo*. I would suggest that Renaissance rhetoric tries to negotiate this dilemma . . . rhetoric seeks to make spiritual reality visible . . . Christian rhetoric, then, operates according to sacramental rather than dialectical modes. It incarnates the spiritual and elicits the affective/intuitive response that can spring from visible sign to invisible reality.[32]

This is all very well, provided that rhetoric is seen as, in some way, the handmaid of faith. Furthermore, it does not reckon with the peculiar demands which the liturgical situation in church places upon religious language.

Shuger's claims for an alliance between faith and rhetoric fail to allow for the ancient tradition in Greek thought, much older than Plato, which attached extremely negative associations to the notion of faith, or 'πίστις', understood as mental conviction. In his book *The Discovery of the Mind* (1953), Bruno Snell compares human and divine knowledge, quoting Heraclitus, 'Human nature has no knowledge, but the divine nature has.'[33] The contrast is made between divine knowledge (ἐπιστήμη) of truth (ἀλήθεια) and human belief (πίστις) about opinion (δόξα). In different ways Homer, Xenophanes, Heraclitus, Parmenides, Empedocles and finally Plato himself den-igrate belief in opinion as opposed to clear knowledge of the truth. Plato in the *Gorgias*, the *Phaedrus* and the *Republic* vividly explores the inferiority of belief which is subject to the powerful manipulation of rhetoric, so apparently indifferent to truth and morality. Finally, in the Christian era, the long battle with gnosticism focused once again the conflict between knowledge and faith and encouraged the Christian denial that its 'notion of an honorific belief system and level of knowledge could hardly have come from the Greeks'.[34]

It is all the more startling, therefore, to discover that Cranmer's rhetoric is profoundly classical, that, indeed, the broader formation of the Christian liturgy is steeped in the classical act of persuasion. With Plato we may, perhaps, have reason to be fearful. Words central in the tradition of doctrine or belief, like 'πίστις' or 'δόξα' may be undergoing a curious religious collapse in the liturgical context, just as words lost their meaning, as Thucydides incisively records, under the stress of the Peloponnesian Wars.[35]

This is not to suggest that Archbishop Cranmer himself was furtively and intentionally engaged in some dark rhetorical plot to coerce a submissive Church. Rather, that he was working with tricky stuff, language, whose devices and traditions may be effective in ways quite distinct from the religious or authorial intentions of the writer. Character and community may, in the end, be defined and made real in performances of language and one is never quite sure, in human terms, of the nature of any authoritative claims which may therein be operative. The community which really matters in the 1549 liturgy is not the ideal community of the Church which celebrates the sacrament, nor even the struggling, confessing community of sinners who offer their 'bounden duetie and seruice', but a 'textual community' constituted in the *aptum* between Cranmer, his congregation – and the language and its content.

In the text, above all, of the 1549 'Supper of the Lord and the Holy Communion', the community perceives its identity and experiences its 'entextualisation'. The very power which the language exerts in its rhetoric constitutes not merely a rehearsal of theological conformity, but a breaking down and reconstituting of language deeper and more recondite than is allowed by the extrinsic claims of recognised spirituality and theology. In the words of James Boyd White in his book *When Words Lose Their Meaning* (1984), 'the language thus remade has a special kind of richness and power that derives from the associate way that it is put together in the text'.[36] In fact, James Boyd White's commentary on the rhetoric of so-called Socratic 'argument' is strikingly similar to the effect of the 1549 liturgy.

> The language so made is powerful, in a sense un-answerable, in large part because it does not seek to eliminate but accepts and clarifies the variabilities and complexities and inconsistencies of ordinary life and language. It is a language not merely of theory, for it has something of poetry in it too, of literature, and a language so made cannot be refuted by simply

disproving one or another point. One must respond to it as a whole. Indeed, the only true refutation would be the creation of a better alternative . . . [The text] works on [the reader] in large part by isolating and disorientating him, by creating a conscious gap between self and language that makes the nature of both problematic in new ways . . . The reader is broken out of his culture, out of the language and activities that define him; he is thus prevented from defining himself by simply repeating established forms of speech or conduct. He is forced to function on his own . . .[37]

The claims of the language of the liturgy are similarly absolute and intolerant of refutation. It is an active, not a theoretical language, disorientating the 'reader' whose very isolation is a threat, casting him back upon the submissive, meek community, bound together by the necessity of the rhetoric. Thus in the Prayer of Oblation in the 1549 Canon, the 'partakers of this Holy Communion' offer themselves to the Lord as a 'sacrifice'. At the same time, they pray that they may worthily receive the sacrament and 'be fulfilled with thy grace and heauenly benediction'. However, they proceed to admit that they are, in fact, unworthy to offer the sacrifice ('through our manyfold synnes'), and so they beseech the Lord to accept what is their duty and service, 'not waying our merites but pardoning our offences'.[38]

Constructed from a patchwork of biblical and liturgical sources this prayer very subtly traps its reader in a necessity which creates 'a conscious gap between self and language'. That which is offered is actually unworthy, yet God is besought to accept the gift which is acceptable only by his grace and pardon. Everything conspires to isolate and undermine each individual, yet each can do no other than contribute to the common act.

In examining the text of 1549 in this way, we have been exploring what Jürgen Habermas calls the 'communicative action' which 'mediates between the ritually preserved fund of social solidarity and existing norms and personal identities'.[39] In fact, the linguistic and rhetorical activity present in the text, apart from the intention of the text's author or the 'intention' of the community, combine with certain 'necessities' in the textual situation, that is the need for solidarity and the pressure to conform (for example, from the politically imposed Act of Uniformity), systematically to distort communication. This devious action of a crucial text in the formation and maintenance of a religious community may be a key to understand what David Klemm has called 'the pseudo-normality, that is the hidden pathology, of collective behaviour and entire social systems'.[40] Insofar as a community will tend to identify and preserve itself by a process of entextua-lisation, so the crucial text will begin to exert its own authority over the community – it becomes a sacred text – and the community can do no other than submit to it. Community of belief then becomes a necessity,[41] and truth merely contingent. In the words of the priest in Kafka's *The Trial*:

> ' . . . it is not necessary to accept everything as true, one must only accept it as necessary'. 'A melancholy conclusion,' said K. 'it turns lying into a universal principle.'[42]

Underlying Socrates' fear of rhetoric is the question, how should we live, and what best equips us for the good life? Such proper concern lies also at the heart of the religious community and its sacred texts. But Socrates' fear is hinted at even in the opening sentence of the Preface to the 1549 Prayer Book: 'There was never anything by the wit of man so well deuised, or so surely established, which (in continuance of time) hath not been corrupted'.[43] At the heart of the text lies a rhetorical and linguistic corruption, evidence of the real nature of the ambiguous relationship between community and the sacred, to which it owes its existence, whose necessity it requires and from which it has everything to fear. And is it true, or merely necessary? Perhaps, indeed, the Fall was originally a linguistic catastrophe, corruption within the heart of the language itself. This suggestion is the subject of the next chapter.

Notes

1. René Girard, *Violence and the Sacred*. Trans. Patrick Gregory. (Baltimore and London, 1977) p. 267.
2. See, Peter Mack, 'Rhetoric and Liturgy', in, David Jasper and R.C.D. Jasper (Eds.), *Language and the Worship of the Church* (London, 1990) pp. 82–3.
3. George A. Kennedy, *Classical Rhetoric and its Christian and Secular Tradition from Ancient to Modern Times* p. 8.
4. See further, G.E. Duffield (Ed.), *The Work of Thomas Cranmer* (Appleford, 1964) pp. 341–65.
5. Chaim Perelman, *The Realm of Rhetoric* p. 7.
6. Ibid. p. 9.
7. See also, James L. Kinneavy, *Greek Rhetorical Origins of Christian Faith* (Oxford, 1987) pp. 33–4.
8. See, Perelman op. cit. p. 95.
9. Jacques-Bénigne Bossuet, *Sermons* Trans. William Kluback (Paris, 1942) II, 'Sur la soumission due à la parole de Jesus-Christ', pp. 117–21.
10. Jacques Derrida, 'White Mythology: Metaphor in the Text of Philosophy' *New Literary History* 6 (1974) 5–74.
11. Cicero, *De Inventione* 1.4.5. See, Brian Vickers, *In Defence of Rhetoric* (Oxford, 1988) pp. 10–11.
12. From, Act of Uniformity 1549. Quoted in C.W. Dugmore, 'The First Ten years, 1549–59', in *The English Prayer Book. 1549–1662* (London, 1963) p. 9.
13. For parallels between the *Consultation* and 1549, see F.E. Brightman, *The English Rite* (London, 1915) Vol. I, pp. xcviii–ciii.
14. See further, R.T. Beckwith, 'The Anglican Eucharist: From the Reformation to the Restoration', in Cheslyn Jones, Geoffrey Wainwright, Edward Yarnold S.J. (Eds.), *The Study of Liturgy* (London, 1978) pp. 264–5.
15. *Cranmer's Selected Writings*, Ed. C.S. Meyer (London, 1961) pp. 90–1. See also, David L. Frost, *The Language of Series 3* (Bramcote, 1973) pp. 5–7 'The Cranmerian Ideal'.
16. Kennedy, op. cit. p. 123.
17. Lamy, *The Art of Speaking* 2.51. Quoted in Debora K. Shuger, *Sacred Rhetoric. The Christian Grand Style in the English Renaissance* (Princeton, 1988) pp. 106–7.
18. Shuger, op. cit. p. 109.

19. See Ibid. p. 223.
20. Girard, op. cit. p. 267.
21. Ibid. p. 268.
22. W.K. Wimsatt Jr., 'The Intentional Fallacy' in W.K. Wimsatt Jr. and Monroe C. Beardsley, *The Verbal Icon. Studies in the Meaning of Poetry* (Lexington, 1954) p. 5.
23. See, Vickers, op. cit. pp. 261–3.
24. C.S. Lewis, *Poetry and Prose in the Sixteenth Century* (Oxford, 1954) p. 61.
25. Stella Brook, *The Language of the Book of Common Prayer* (London, 1965) is almost completely silent on the subject of rhetoric.
26. In, R.C.D. Jasper (Ed.) *The Eucharist Today* (London, 1974) pp. 142–67.
27. See, Mack, op. cit. pp. 83, 89. Generally, see H. Lausberg, *Handbuch der literarischen Rhetorik*. 2 Vols. (Munich, 1960).
28. See, Mack, op. cit. p. 95.
29. Brightman, Vol. II, p. 650.
30. Ibid. pp. 696–7. A translation of the *Consultation* is printed in G.J. Cuming, *A History of Anglican Liturgy*. 2nd Ed. (London, 1982) pp. 286–304.
31. See further, A.C. Clark, *Prose Rhythm in English* (Oxford, 1913): G.C. Richards, 'Coverdale and the Cursus'. *Church Quarterly Review*, 219 (April, 1930) 34–9: Kennedy, op. cit. p. 186: Mack op. cit. pp. 97, 103.
32. Shuger, op. cit. p. 227. See further, Klaus Dockhorn, 'Rhetoric movet: Protestantischer Humanismus und Karolingische Renaissance', in, Helmut Schanze (Ed.), *Rhetorik: Beitrage zu ihrer Geschichte in Deutschland vom 16–20 Jahrhundert* (Frankfurt, 1974) pp. 17–42.
33. Bruno Snell, *The Discovery of the Mind: The Greek Origins of European Thought*. Trans. T.G. Rosemeyer (Oxford, 1953) p. 136. See also, Kinneavy, op. cit. pp. 17–20.
34. Kinneavy, op. cit. p. 20.
35. See, Thucydides, *History of the Peloponnesian War*, 3.82 ff. Also, James Boyd White, *When Words Lose Their Meaning. Constitutions and Reconstituion of Language. Characters and Community.* (Chicago and London, 1984) p. 3.
36. James Boyd White, op. cit. p. 107.
37. Ibid. pp. 108–9.
38. Brightman, op. cit. Vol. II, p. 694.
39. Jürgen Habermas, *The Theory of Communicative Action*. Trans. Thomas McCarthy (Cambridge, 1987) Vol. II. p. 77.
40. David E. Klemm, *Hermeneutical Inquiry*, Vol. II: *The Interpretation of Existence* (Atlanta, 1986) p. 210.
41. See, Stanley Fish, *Is there a Text in This Class? The Authority of Interpretive Communities* (Harvard, 1980) p. 365.
42. Franz Kafka, *The Trial* 1925. Trans. Willa and Edwin Muir (Harmondsworth, 1971) p. 243.
43. Brightman, op. cit. Vol. I, p. 34.

6

'Verbs Conjugated Sweetly, Verse Began': Bakhtin's Contribution

They spoke the loveliest of languages.
Their tongues entwined in Persian, ran
And fused. Words kissed, a phrase embraced,
Verbs conjugated sweetly. Verse began.
So Eve and Adam lapped each other up
The livelong day, the lyric night.

Of all known tongues most suasive
Was the Snake's. His oratory was Arabic,
Whose smile and rhetoric seduced her
('Sovran of creatures, universal dame').
So potent its appeal –
The apple asked for eating,
To eat it she was game.

Now Gabriel turned up, the scholars say,
Shouting in Turkish. Harsh and menacing,
But late. And sounds like swords were swung.
Fault was underlined, and crime defined.
The gate slammed with the clamour of his tongue.

Eden was gone. A lot of other things
Were won. Or done. Or suffered.
Thorns and thistles, dust and dearth.
The words were all before them, which to choose.
Their tongues now turned to English,

With its colonies of twangs.
And they were down to earth.[1]

In D. J. Enright's poem 'History of World Languages', the
fall in Eden is perceived as a linguistic catastrophe. The
very order and syntax of language – its conjugations,
structured and obediently learned by students and
scholars seeking system, leads to verse and worse. Rhetoric persuades and is the instrument of seduction, and
human free will is the place of entrapment – game Eve
plays the game and becomes the game. Strengthened by
the poetic skill of rhetoric, words slide between meanings
– which to choose? – defy meaning, and we are caught.
As Enright himself remarks in his book *The Alluring
Problem* (1988) on his childhood pity for the green hill far
away deprived of a city wall and, as itself a victim of
injustice, an appropriate venue for the crucifixion, 'I misunderstood, there as elsewhere, but I was captured; and
to be captured is more important than to understand.'[2]
    Words are powerful and dangerous precisely insofar
as, sinuously snakelike, they slither between meanings,
and, since the work of Ferdinand de Saussure early in
this century, fundamental questions have multiplied
concerning semantic integration: from the arbitrariness
of the sign, the problem emerges where to locate the seat
of control directing meaning in language.[3] For where
meaning is lost, arbitrary power – the brute force of
rhetoric – stakes its claim and, in Habermas' graphic
phrase, 'discourses emerge and pop like glittering bubbles
from a swamp of anonymous processes of subjugation'.[4]
No-one knows better than the poet the bewitchment of
language – not the theologian, nor the philosopher, poor
systematic fools! That is why Plato feared the artists, and
wished to banish them from his Republic. And so that
most dour of our modern poets, almost crippled (like
Gerard Manley Hopkins) by his knowledge of the sin of
language and its alluring beauty, Geoffrey Hill wrote

(1989) in the *Times Literary Supplement* of the volumes of the new second edition of *The Oxford English Dictionary*:

> To brood over them and in them is to be finally persuaded that sematology is a theological dimension: the use of language is inseparable from that 'terrible aboriginal calamity' in which, according to Newman, the human race is implicated . . . In what sense or senses is the computer acquainted with original sin?[5]

The presentation of words as interconnected in a dictionary, each word defined by other words, suggests something of the anonymity of language as a system.[6] The question then remains, is this structure of inter-con-nectedness the whole of language? Are words grounded, somehow, in the Word, or is our senseless discourse merely a swamp which entraps us and finally drowns us? That question is a serious one in modern literature, and not simply reserved for those who appear to indulge in the Derridian excesses of post-modernity. The Canadian novelist Malcolm Lowry published his hellish vision, *Under the Volcano* in 1947 – a profound meditation on the battle with language, at the end of which is only 'the inconceivable pandemonium'[7] of madness and deafening, silent screams. One thinks also of the nightmare pictures of the artist Edvard Munch. Ten years earlier, in 1937, Lowry wrote to his friend Conrad Aiken:

> Dear old bird:
> Have now reached condition of amnesia, breakdown, heartbreak, consumption, cholera, alcoholic poisoning, and God will not like to know what else, if he has to, which is damned doubtful.
> All change here, all change here, for Oakshot, Cockshot, Poxshot and fuck the whole bloody lot!
> My only friend here is a tertiary who pins a medal of the Virgin of Guadalupe on my coat;

follows me in the street (when I am not in prison, and he followed me there too several times); and who thinks I am Jesus Christ, which, as you know, I am not yet, though I may be progressing towards thinking I am myself.

I have been imprisoned as a spy in a dungeon compared with which the Chateau d'If – in the film – is a little cottage in the country overlooking the sea.

I spent Christmas – New Year's – Wedding Day there. All my mail is late. When it does arrive it is all contradiction and yours is cut into little holes.

Don't think I can go on. Where I am it is dark. Lost.

Happy New Year,
Malcolm.[8]

Languages slides into incoherence, the only mimesis of Lowry's own condition whose hell is to be imprisoned in language – anonymous, non-referential, coldly artistic. And the experience is not just that of the alcoholic reprobate Lowry. Gerard Manley Hopkins, 'one of the most powerful and profound of our religious poets' as one of his editors describes him (and he may be right)[9] could not, in the end, sustain the tension between his poetry and his religious calling. Words slide and slip away from the moorings of meaning and definition. In his diary for September 1863, Hopkins wrote (and we recall Lowry's 'all change here'), '*Grind, gride, gird, grit, groat, grate, greet,* κρόυειν, *crush, crash,* κροτεῖν, etc. Original meaning to *strike, rub* . . .'[10] But the original meaning, if there ever was such a paradisial linguistic condition, is swallowed up in a kaleidoscope of words which, in the power of their interconnectedness defy reference until, in the demonic brilliance of Hopkins' late 'terrible' sonnets, the discipline of the poet itself reveals the abyss of language.

                                         And my lament
Is cries countless, cries like dead letters sent
To dearest him that lives alas! away.[11]

Hopkins was a victim of the original sin of language. He
could not be a poet and a priest. Yet the Church has made
a ghastly icon of him, most obscenely presented in the
chapter on Hopkins in Hans Urs von Balthasar's *The
Glory of the Lord*. Part III (1962), in which his violent
struggle with language is falsely clothed in the comforts
of Christian doctrine ('death as Resurrection'), the unbearable allurements of conjugating verbs apparently
encouraging in him a distasteful religious voyeurism ('he
can catch an almost naked glimpse of the love of God').[12]
Actually, in his last years in Dublin Hopkins was closer
to the Inferno of Lowry's *Under the Volcano*.

    Debate concerning the referential status of the linguistic
sign is by no means limited to our own time in the history
of Western philosophy. Heraclitus, among the pre-Socratic
philosophers, sought to establish the 'naturalness' of
names, finding in them traces of primal wisdom. But
against such claims for 'linguistic infallibility', proponents
of linguistic conventionalism asserted that a sign and its
referent are merely accidentally related – witness the
variety of languages, 'after Babel' as it were, designating
the same object in different ways. Aristotle himself in the
De Interpretatione gives the classic statement of this view:

A noun signifies this or that by convention (κατὰ
συνθήκην). No sound is by nature a noun, it becomes
one, becoming a symbol . . . Every sentence has meaning, though not as an instrument of nature (φύσει) but,
as we observed, by convention.[13]

According to Aristotle, words are not 'natural' and bear
no relation or contiguity to the thing signified. At best
they are socially determined, and Aristotle does not deal

with the obvious question of how linguistic usage comes to be established in the first place. His account of language it seems is purely functional.[14]

It is precisely such a view of linguistic conventionalism which structuralist and post-structuralist linguistics have adopted and developed. The arbitrariness of language makes language ultimately self-defining, whole and complete. Above all it is self-regulating and appeals to no 'reality' beyond itself.[15] And what Saussure begins in his *Cours de Linguistique Générale* (1915), Derrida completes in *Of Grammatology* (1967), which is to conclude the project of Nietzsche – 'the liberation of the signifier from its dependence or derivation with respect to the logos and the related concept of truth or the primary signified'.[16] It is precisely at this moment, when language revels in the moment of ontological destruction, and the notion of truth itself is held in question, that rhetoric comes into its own, proposing and promoting the deceptive utilisation of an absolute set within the prolongation of a myth.[17]

What I mean is this. Rhetoric, the art of persuasion, works not from ontology but from a form of argumentation, and, as Aristotle recognised, in the Babel of opinions, argumentation may be powerful in its claims upon us even although its truth is evasive. We return again to Perelman's thesis that the argument works not from premise but towards consent in the community to a given thesis or theses.[18] Its concern is the establishment of an unavoidable authority.

Rhetoric is an art of language, an element of artifice and ingenuity in language polished and heightened beyond our 'normal' habits of speech,[19] concerned with the exercise of interest and ideology, not truth, and by its very discipline powerful enough to release the dangerous, self-defining artitrariness of words and syntax. It is no accident that rhetoric is once again, in Klemm's words, 'on the curriculum for the study of theology',[20] since in an age of postmodernism, metaphysical theology has shifted to hermeneutical theology which recognises the apparent contradiction between the increasingly elusive subject matter of theology and argumentation as such. Hermeneutics plays the mercurial role of mediating between the intolerable presence of confessional theology (which recognises no gap between God and symbol of God) and the seemingly desolate absence of deconstructive theology (which admits no relation between them).[21] The apparent freedom of this interpretative, hermeneutic exercise depends upon a central theological metaphor for God, that is, the breaking-in of otherness.[22] The dominant nineteenth-century claim of God as absolute knowledge disintegrated as World War I fractured the sense of continuity between human existence and the being of God, and it was, perhaps, above all Rudolf Otto's book *The Idea of the Holy* (1917) which seriously introduced the new paradigm, perfectly available in our climate of disunity and fragmentation.

Why is this so? Rudolf Bultmann saw the point as long ago as 1925 in his essay 'What does it mean to speak of God?'[23] Bultmann begins by making the asserting that 'if "speaking of God" is understood as *"speaking about God"*, then such speaking has no meaning whatever, for its subject, God, is lost in the very moment it takes place'.[24] Theological argumentation, then, cannot be carried out in the form of the theistic argument for the existence of a supreme being. The conviction that 'God is' is reached only in terms of appearance and interpretation of otherness – a radical otherness whose very nature is to be other, even other than itself. Hence, in Klemm's beautifully insistent words:

What breaks in as God is not, strictly speaking, God. What breaks in must be the appearance, symbol or manifestation of God – hence God in its otherness as word or language. Consequently, in current theology, the most basic statement made about God is that 'God

is God as word'. God breaks in as otherness in word
. . . God breaks in as what is other than God. What
breaks in is word, the otherness of God, which is also
the medium of our thinking and being and hence
in some sense familiar, albeit normally hidden or
forgotten.[25]

But what are the consequences of this for theological
argument? Actually, that theological argument affirms
that 'God is' by arguing against the possibility of a
logically sound argument for the existence of God. Argumentation, in other words, works best as argument which
undercuts the possibility of argument – and this is precisely the condition in which rhetoric flourishes and the
formalist qualities of language are most powerful (unless
outflanked by irony). Why? Because the hermeneutic circle is powerfully asserted by the metaphor of in-breaking
of otherness which *appears* to contradict and smash it, but
cannot do so since the otherness is always other than
itself. The rhetoric successfully dupes its audience into
belief in nothing but the self-defining, self-regulating
power of language on a vertical axis.

   We are caught by what Paul Ricoeur calls 'a sort of
twist on the words'.[26] Is this all we can hope for? In the
course of my reflections I shall try to suggest that this is
not so, but for now confronted by this frightening spectre
of theological argument, with words in their element of
power compressed by art, we need to face the crucial
question asked by Bakhtin; who in any given act is responsible? I refer to Mikhail Bakhtin, and will devote
much of the remainder of this chapter to his work,
because as a Russian intellectual in the twenties and until
his death in 1975 he was strongly influenced by the Christianity of the Russian Orthodox Church (probably the
main cause of his period of exile under Stalin in the
1930s), and struggled with the political questions of
authority and responsibility in the Soviet Union, and

particularly under Stalin's dictatorship. The two matters are closely related.

Bakhtin vigorously opposed the linguistic formalism of leading (and politically favoured) scholars like Roman Jakobson and Viktor Shklovsky. Art, they argued, was autonomous: a permanent, self-determining, continuous human activity which warranted nothing less than examination in and on its own terms.[27] Self-consciously a-political, most of the leading Formalists moved to the top of the cultural hierarchy in Moscow in the 1920s, and not by accident.[28] For their linguistic principles tended towards the production of a rhetoric which beautifully sustained an authoritarian ideology perceived in quasi-theological terms, on a vertical axis which professed an inbreaking of beneficent authority, but actually embraced a static, unified version of society which can make no moral claims outside its own structures.

Probably Bakhtin's greatest work is entitled *Rabelais and His World* (1965), composed in the teeth of the Stalinist repression. Rabelais (1494?–c. 1553), author of the *Pantagruel* and *Gargantua*, is the epic poet of sheer physicality, drawing deeply upon popular culture, the grotesque, the comic, 'carnival', revelling in the joys of endless food and tireless sex. He is, in Bakhtin's term, a 'deeply revolutionary spirit'.[29] In what sense? Well, Bakhtin identifies three political villains which threatened the culture of France of Rabelais' time. The first villain is the bourgeoisie (in the best Marxist–Leninist tradition). The second is the Holy Roman Empire and its hegemony (compare with it Stalin's repression of nationalist movements in the USSR). The third, and principal villain is the Roman Catholic Church, with its oppression of the lower classes, its 'dry scholasticism', its cult of the priests and 'obscurantism'. Above all, the Church is attacked for its role as self-proclaimed 'sole possessor of the truth'. From whence actually does its authority come?

As with the linguistic formalism of Jakobson and his colleagues, the Church's discourse is always caught up

with a power which may be by no means benign.[30] And
Bakhtin's critique of the medieval Roman Catholic Church
spills over in his critique of Stalinism, with respect to its
fundamental epistemological principle, that is the vertical
ordering of all reality and its 'vertical world' of absolute
values,[31] reflected in the structures of the Church's
hierarchy. Bakhtin puts it in this way:

> In the medieval picture of the world, the top and bot-
> tom, the higher and lower, have an absolute meaning
> both in the sense of space and of values. Therefore, the
> images of the upward movement, the way of ascent, or
> the symbols of descent or fall played in this system an
> exceptional role, as they did also in the sphere of art
> and literature. Every important movement was seen
> and interpreted only as upward and downward, along
> a vertical line. All metaphors of movement in medieval
> thought and art have this sharply defined, surprisingly
> consistent vertical character.[32]

Under the Church, under Stalin, this vertical model
becomes the perfect instrument for introducing the theological metaphors of the breaking-in of otherness and the
conviction that authority may claim a genuinely revelatory
quality. In fact, the absolute values of the system are the
more powerful in that they arise from a purely formalist
rhetoric, answerable to nothing beyond themselves. Furthermore, it is precisely the syntactical discipline (one
might almost say 'poetic') of such rhetoric which
compresses the arbitrary freedom of language so that
Rabelaisian physical celebration becomes rigidly defined
in the 'correct' language of orthodoxy as both obscenity
and sin.

Out of such order come notions of sin and wickedness:

> Obscenity [writes Bakhtin] has become narrowly sexual,
> isolated, individual, and has no place in the new

official system of philosophy and imagery . . . The
sense of the body that is celebrated in carnival is now
restricted too: Anything that protrudes, bulges, sprouts,
or branches off . . . is eliminated, hidden, moderated
. . . This restricted sense of the body is accompanied by
restraints on speech: the verbal forms of official and
literary language, determined by the canon, prohibit
all that is linked with fecundation, pregnancy, child-
birth. There is a sharp dividing line between familiar
speech and 'correct' language.[33]

The terrible discipline of ideological rhetoric releases the
original sin of language. Against this, Bakhtin sets a carnival world that is organised horizontally,[34] opposed to
all hierarchies in epistemology and whose essential
qualities are incompleteness, becoming and ambiguity.
In this world 'there is no last word', and language, ex-
periencing the freedom of its being, actually recovers its
capacity to express the inner nature of the things it desig-
nates, recovers the referentiality it lost in Eden.

Nakedness again is simply nakedness and not rude or
immoral.

One of the great moments in English dramatic literature
recognises the tragic loss of the linguistic innocence of
carnival as it is defined by the sententious moralism of
adopted, authoritarian rhetoric. At the end of Shakespeare's *Henry IV, Part II*, Prince Hal, newly
elevated to the dignity of his throne, thrusts aside his
former companion and playmate, Falstaff:

I know thee not, old man. Fall to thy prayers.
How ill white hairs become a fool and jester!
I have long dreamed of such a kind of man,
So surfeit-swelled, so old, and so profane,
But, being awaked, I do despise my dream.[35]

It is more than sad, it is nauseating, and nothing in Falstaff
is profane except authority makes it so. Life, carnival,

companionship, laughter is replaced by the vaunted language of *Henry V*, a play useful, it was found, to encourage young Englishmen in 1940 (as at Agincourt and Harfleur) to hate their enemies and lay down their lives; while Falstaff, meanwhile, dies in Eden's fields:

> Nay sure, he's not in hell: he's in Arthur's bosom if ever man went to Arthur's bosom: a' made a finer end, and went away an it had been any christom child: a' parted e'en just between twelve and one, e'en at the turning o'th' tide; for after I saw him fumble with the sheets, and play with flowers, and smile upon his finger's end, I knew there was but one way: for his nose was a sharp as a pen, and a' babbled of green fields.[36]

All that I have been trying to say relates closely to the argument put forward by Elaine Pagels in her book *Adam, Eve and the Serpent* (1988). She is engaging essentially in an enquiry into the nature of original sin – how the Christian tradition came to find sexual desire sinful, how infants are corrupted with original sin and Adam's sin corrupted the whole of nature. How did the Christian church, proclaiming the value and freedom of the individual, come to insist that humankind cannot choose not to sin?

Inevitably the politics of Paradise must recognise the large role here played by St Augustine, but Professor Pagels crucially insists upon the effect throughout the Christian tradition of the arts of language and rhetoric – the art of persuasion which is a corruption in the very means of communicating the action of grace. She considers the writings of John Chrysostom, who envisages the paradisial condition of the Christian church as opposed to the secular Empire of his day. 'There [in the Empire] everything is done through fear and constraint; here [in the church], through free choice and liberty.'[37] Nevertheless the priest's authority, far from being inferior, in fact *surpasses* that of the emperor, for the priest guides the sinner whom he leads 'back by persuasion to the truth from which he originally swerved'.[38] Each church member's voluntary participation is achieved by the arts of persuasion – and, alas, Chrysostom remains uncomfortably aware that the actual church on earth falls far short of the original harmony of Paradise within which alone such persuasion may truly operate within a voluntary environment. And so disorder follows, and 'the disorder has taken on a kind of method and consistency of its own'.[39] Is such the birth of systematic theology? Eden was gone, the words were all before them, which to choose. Only those, I suggest, which work effectively, powerfully, define for us the obscene, are believed; and feared: and for them we take no responsibility, but blame God, or Adam – the inbreaking on the vertical axis. And so Eve says (as D.J. Enright informs us):

> I'm glad it wasn't me
> Who named them.[40]

The arts of language compound and promote the necessary organisation which must ensue once the freedom of Paradise has been lost upon the persuasive, brilliant, powerful rhetoric of the serpent (by far the best theologian in Milton's *Paradise Lost*). Not the argument itself but the authority which it presents is the real concern of this art, which, as Socrates warns, is a vaunted device, an instrument of deception, falsifying reality and any notion of truth.[41]

It is the hardened fixity of the written word which is for Socrates an obstacle in the path of truth, for that fixity allows the autonomous, non-referential arbitrariness of language to define moral limits outside a properly referential context. Theological language then may, in Ray L. Hart's words, *'illustrate* "original sin" through its preoccupation with God in the way that only God can be preoccupied with himself'.[42]

In response to this, what Bakhtin proposes is an art and language built of impurities, the art of the novel as described in his book *Problems of Dostoyevsky's Poetics* (1984). It is an art which is unfinished and revels in 'heteroglossia', which responds to the fundamental joys of incarnation and human inter-subjectivity: which is therefore linked referentially to the experience which gives rise to it. Words then may bite once more upon the substance of their reference, and do not become self-absorbed. For we recall such dangers of self-absorption in the history of world languages: 'Words kissed, a phrase embraced. Verbs conjugated sweetly. Verse began.'

But if we are brought, in our postmodern condition, to a new beginning for theological discourse – a horizontal, comic and ironic discourse, without fixity, in a new freedom and innocence of language, we also return to that fundamental question which needs to be asked, again with Bakhtin; who, if anybody, is responsible for the semantic weight of any given statement? Who in any given act is responsible, God's law, man's will, or the naughty play of a system of linguistic signs?

Notes

1. D.J. Enright, 'History of World Language'. *Collected Poems 1987.* (Oxford, 1987) p. 206.
2. D.J. Enright, *The Alluring Problem. An Essay on Irony.* (Oxford, 1988; first publ. 1986) pp. 58–9.
3. See, Katerina Clark and Michael Holquist, *Mikhail Bakhtin* (Harvard, 1984) p. 81.
4. Jürgen Habermas, *The Philosophical Discourse of Modernity.* Trans. Frederick Lawrence. (Cambridge, 1987) p. 268.
5. Geoffrey Hill, review of *The Oxford English Dictionary.* 2nd Ed. *TLS* April 21–27, 1989. p. 414.
6. See, David E. Klemm, 'The Rhetoric of Theological Argument', in Nelson, Megill, and McCloskey (Eds.), *The Rhetoric of the Human Sciences* (Wisconsin, 1987) p. 290.
7. Malcolm Lowry, *Under the Volcano.* (Harmondsworth, 1963; first publ. 1947) p. 376.
8. Harvey Breit and Margerie Bonner Lowry (Eds.), *Selected Letters of Malcolm Lowry* (Harmondsworth, 1985) p. 80.
9. W.H. Gardner, in Gerard Manley Hopkins, *Poems and Prose.* (Harmondsworth, 1953) p. xiii.

10. Ibid. p. 90.
11. G.M. Hopkins, 'I wake and feel the fell of dark not day.' Ibid. p. 62.
12. Hans Urs von Balthasar, *The Glory of the Lord, Part III: Studies in Theological Style: Lay Styles.* (Edinburgh, 1986; first publ. 1962) pp. 398–9.
13. Aristotle, *De interpretatione* 16a. 26, 17a.1. Quoted in James C. McKusick, Coleridge's *Philosophy of Language* (Yale, 1986; first publ. 1967) p. 6.
14. See also, McKusick, op. cit. pp. 4 ff.
15. See, Terence Hawkes, *Structuralism and Semiotics* (London, 1977) pp. 25 ff.
16. Jacques Derrida, *Of Grammatology* (Baltimore, 1976; first pub. 1967) p. 19.
17. See, Chaim Perelman, *The Realm of Rhetoric* p. 125.
18. See above Chapter 5, pp. 82–3.
19. See, Peter Dixon, *Rhetoric*, p. 3.
20. David E. Klemm, 'Toward a Rhetoric of Postmodern Theology: Through Barth and Heidegger', p. 443. See also below Chapter 7 pp. 109–10.
21. Ibid. p. 462.
22. See, David E. Klemm, 'The Rhetoric of Theological Argument'. pp. 278 ff.
23. Rudolf Bultmann, *Faith and Understanding* (London, 1969) pp. 53–65.
24. Ibid. p. 53.
25. Klemm, 'The Rhetoric of Theological Argument'. p. 280. See also above Chapter 4, p. 65.
26. Paul Ricoeur, *Interpretation Theory: Discourse and the Surplus of Meaning* (Fort Worth, 1976) p. 50.
27. See, Hawkes, op. cit. pp. 59–73.
28. See, Clark and Holquist, op. cit. p. 36.
29. Ibid. p. 295: Bakhtin, *Rabelais and His World* Trans. Helene Iswolsky (Bloomington, 1984) pp. 3 ff.
30. See, Terry Eagleton, *Literary Theory: An Introduction* (Oxford, 1983) p. 73.
31. Bakhtin, *Rabelais and His World* pp. 401–2.
32. Ibid., p. 401.
33. *Rabelais and His World.* pp. 109, 320, 433: Clark and Holquist, op. cit. p. 320.
34. *Rabelais and His World*, p. 397.
35. Shakespeare, *King Henry IV, Part II.* V. 5. 48–52.
36. Shakespeare, *Henry V.* II. 3. 9–16.
37. Elaine Pagels, *Adam, Eve and the Serpent* (London, 1988) p. 103.
38. Chrysostom, *De sacerdotis.* 2, 3: Pagels, op. cit. 103–4.
39. Chrysostom, *Homiliae in Epistolam ad Ephesios.* 6, 7.
40. D.J. Enright, *Paradise Illustrated: A Sequence.* XXIV. *Collected Poems.* p. 191.
41. Dixon, op. cit. p. 11.
42. Ray L. Hart, *Unfinished Man and the Imagination* (Atlanta, 1985) p. 38.

7

Theology and the New Rhetoric: Shepherding the Sheep or Pulling the Wool over their Eyes?

> . . . up rose
> Belial in act more graceful and humane;
> A fairer person lost not Heav'n; he seem'd
> For dignity compos'd and high exploit:
> But all was false and hollow; though his Tongue
> Dropt Manna, and could make the worse appear
> The better reason, to perplex and dash
> Maturest counsels: for his thoughts were low; . . .
> . . . yet he pleas'd the ear,
> And with persuasive accents thus began.

> (*Paradise Lost*, II, 108–15, 117–18)

Here, with consummate rhetoric, Milton assembles the traditional arguments against rhetoric. Drawing attention to his appearance, his superficiality, Belial acts his part in a series of double meanings – all false and hollow. His seeming honesty is a lie 'to perplex and dash/Maturest counsels', yet highly persuasive. As Socrates declares in the *Gorgias*, 'There is no need for rhetoric to know the facts at all, for it has hit upon a means of persuasion that enables it to appear in the eyes of the ignorant to know more than those who really know' (459).[1] Rhetoric, it would appear, as we have seen so often in this book, is deficient epistemologically (neglecting truth and fact), morally (neglecting true knowledge and sincerity), and socially. In fact, it encourages people to behave badly.

Of course, just as there is traditional argument against rhetoric, there are also the standard defences, usually stemming from Aristotle. But as rhetoric increasingly returns to the agenda of discipline after discipline and scholars are encouraged to reflect upon the rhetorical nature of their writing, the suspicion grows that Milton was right to fear Satanic rhetoric, and that caution should be exercised. Let me illustrate my suspicion with reference to a non-theological text concerned with this subject, Donald McCloskey's *The Rhetoric of Economics* (1985), which affirms that rhetoric deals not with abstract truth, but with truth that emerges only in the context of distinctly human conversations, and that 'there is no reason to search for a general quality called Truth'.[2] The real truth, he concludes, is that 'assertions are made for the purposes of persuading some audience', and 'given the unavailability of a God's-eye view, "that is not a shameful fact", but the bottom line fact in a rhetorical world'.[3]

It was a point made by I.A. Richards, that questions of value and meaning are finally rhetorical, and that, as Isocrates observes, good discourse is discourse that works. The consequences are not pleasant to contemplate, and are well illustrated by Stanley Fish in an essay on Freud's *The Wolf Man*. Fish begins with an allusion to James Strachey's preface to his translation of Freud's *Introductory Lectures*, which claims that Freud was 'never rhetorical' and was entirely opposed to laying down his view in an authoritarian fashion. Fish continues with 'a report by the Wolf-Man of what he thought to himself shortly after he met Freud for the first time: this man is a Jewish swindler, he wants to use me from behind and shit on my head'.[4] The Wolf-Man, of course, was right in his way, since the 'primal scene' of the wolf dream is not recovered in analysis, but constructed – it is a rhetorical object, and 'it is the definition of a rhetorical object that it is entirely constructed and stands without external support'.[5] At bottom, the primal scene is the scene of persuasion, and the one thing you cannot do in relation to persuasion is get to the bottom of it, since, assuming the stance of rhetorician, it underwrites everything, particularly any efforts to elude it. Any ambitious Freudian coming-from-behind seems, therefore, rather an act of sneaky sodomy.

In economics, in psychoanalysis, an anti-essentialism appears to underlie rhetorical thinking, confirmed again in the hermeneutic and 'edifying' philosophy of Richard Rorty, whose sense of cultural and linguistic contingency seems to commend to us the imperatives and goals already informing our practices. For him, truth, goodness and beauty are to be regarded 'as artifacts whose fundamental design we often have to alter'.[6] There speaks the rhetorical man.

What then of the possibility of a New Rhetoric, a new covenant with language: or is innocence but the dream of a self that is forever fatally flawed?[7] The prophet of the so-called 'New Rhetoric' has been Chaim Perelman whose humanism claims a rationality which is embedded in verbal structures and which justifies philosophical and political pluralism. With Aristotle as his spiritual father, and to a large extent rejecting the formalism which is implicit in my presentation so far, Perelman is prepared to forgo the classical rhetorical theory of demonstration, according to which 'the validity of the deductive method was guaranteed by intuition or evidence – by the natural light of reason'. Instead he appeals to 'dialectical reasoning founded on opinion and concerned with contingent realities'.[8] Such reasoning presupposes a meeting of minds, a distinction between persuasion and compulsion made by the orator, and a disposition to listen on the part of the audience. True, rhetoric may be concerned only with the presentation of a point of view, whereas dialectical discussion is presided over by truth, yet Aristotle's recognition of the similarity between rhetoric and dialectic is, for Perelman, all-important. Indeed, precisely because rhetoric will not identify with the truth, in the singular, though never properly distant from it, it actually provides a justification for the pluralism which the theologian David Tracy has so insisted upon as characteristic of our age.

I find an odd circularity in all this. I am not sure how, in the New Rhetoric, one finally distinguishes a 'good' argument from a 'bad' argument – in which case in what sense is argument useful? And it is, to say the least, odd that Perelman refers with such satisfaction to the rhetorical argument of Mark Antony's great speech over the body of Caesar in Shakespeare's *Julius Caesar* (Act III, Sc. 2), in which, he claims, 'rhetoric becomes a subject of great philosophical interest'.[9] For the speech opens with a funeral eulogy, a typical case of epideictic discourse:

> Friends, Romans, countrymen, lend me your ears;
> I come to bury Caesar, not to praise him;

and concludes by provoking a political riot. Claiming to be reasonable, and identified as such by the crowd ('Methinks there is much reason in his sayings'. I Plebeian), Antony significantly ends his speech:

> O judgment! thou art fled to brutish beasts,
> And men have lost their reason.

Not much philosophy here, but the brutal effect of a powerful, blinding rhetoric. Yet Perelman insists upon the reasonableness of an argument which 'convinces', not from *a priori* necessity, but by drawing the assent of 'an informed, philosophically inclined audience', as one commentator has put it.[10] But actually does this New Rhetoric assume a reasonable audience or create a 'reasonable' audience, like Mark Antony, on its own terms? Perelman certainly believes the former, allowing as it does for pluralism, and asserts that

> All intellectual activity which is placed between the
> necessary and the arbitrary is reasonable to the degree
> that it is maintained by arguments and eventually
> clarified by controversies which normally do not lead
> to unanimity.[11]

But given that his methods are, by his own definition,
rhetorical, by whose validation can he be said to be right?

Perelman rejects 'the guarantee which God gives to
self-evidence',[12] and his New Rhetoric in other respects
poses as a grammar of assent, agreement being reached
by means of what is remarkably similar to Cardinal
Newman's 'illative sense'.[13] John Coulson, a Newman
scholar, has lovingly compared this to the imaginative
assent required by literature, wherein 'the limit of increasing probabilities' becomes 'credibility in the conclusion'.[14] The movement from the probable to the
credible is made not by reason, but, as Newman puts it in
his *Apologia* (1864), by the whole man moving, of which
logic is but the paper record. I am suspicious here when
I view this against the background of rhetorical persuasion, and my suspicion was compounded when I discovered that Bernard Lonergan in his book *Method in
Theology* (1972) adopts Newman's grammar of assent in
terms of the notion of 'conversion', quoting from Newman
with enthusiasm:

> Logic makes but a sorry rhetoric with the multitude;
> first shoot round corners, and you may not despair of
> converting by syllogism.[15]

One is, or ought to be, deeply suspicious of things which
shoot round corners! They tend to knock you flat against
your will.

I sense therefore, in the urbane humanism of Perelman's New Rhetoric, and the Catholicism of Newman's
grammar of assent, a common lurking rhetorical threat:

a grammar, a disciplined use of language which uses its claims of freedom from a certain dry logic to induce assent by shadier forces, when, in Wayne Booth's words, in his work which parallels that of Perelman, *Modern Dogma and the Rhetoric of Assent* (1974), 'the study of the logos as speech leads to faith in the Logos [with a capital L] as ground of speech. But it is in those moments when we move from arguments for or against literal conclusions and express our assents and denials in communal art that our inescapably assenting natures become clearest'.[16]

While locking us within the demands of this new rhetoric, Perelman and Booth continually stake their claim for a middle ground between a somewhat crude notion of cold logic, and irrationality. But in doing so they return us to a rhetorical climate of apparently reasoned argument which contributes ultimately to an 'inescapable assent', which denies the grounds of all argumentation. Freud's Wolf-Man was right, after all.

I do not think it is impossible to occupy this so-called middle ground with a 'logic' which is described by S.T. Coleridge as 'more subtle, more complex, and dependent on more and more fugitive causes'.[17] But my discourse must run a little further yet before I am brought to that particular ground, and as I return again to the rhetoric of religion, in true rhetorical fashion, with Mark Antony I crave that you

... Bear with me;
My heart is in the coffin there with Caesar,
And I must pause till it come back to me. [*he weeps*][18]

As Perelman proclaims a New Rhetoric, and Wayne Booth a rhetoric of assent, so David Klemm makes a case for a contemporary 'rhetoric of theological argument' in a number of his more creative writings, most particularly in three articles, 'The Rhetoric of Theological Argument' (1987), 'Toward a Rhetoric of Postmodern Theology'

(1987), and 'Ricoeur, Theology and the Rhetoric of Overturning' (1989).[19] Klemm begins to establish his 'rhetoric'
by claiming, as I have already briefly noted in Chapter 6,
that unity is to be found in the leading metaphor of God
in contemporary theology: 'God as the breaking-in of
"otherness" to human existence'.[20] From this claim for the
'metaphor of the breaking-in' which 'has been pervasive
and persuasive in theological discussion', as Klemm
would put it, through Barth and Heidegger, he develops
further what might be described as his version of a rhetoric
of assent to otherness by way of a return to the four
master tropes of thought and discourse: metaphor,
metonymy, synecdoche and irony. But as I have suggested before, Klemm's theological affirmation is founded
upon the denial of the possibility of sound argumentation
and is sustained only by a pure formalism which
powerfully asserts a neat hermeneutic circle within which
the rhetoric of persuasion flourishes.

Klemm's further identification of the tropic moment of
synecdoche, in which the elements of metonymic reduction are reassembled or reconstituted into a new figure,
as marking 'the inbreaking of God from outside the linguistic structure'[22] in a humane, not to say urbane, sense
of re-assembly further confirms in his theology a
hermeneutic circle powerfully asserted by the metaphor
of in-breaking of otherness which appears to contradict
and smash it, but cannot do so since the otherness is
always other than itself. This rhetoric draws its audience
towards assenting to and believing in nothing but the
formal and self-involved power of the endlessly energetic
linguistic structure.

In his latest essay on the subject, 'Ricoeur, Theology
and the Rhetoric of Overturning', Klemm reasserts his
position by proposing that 'the intention of the rhetoric of
overturning is to give us hope for transfigured freedom'.[23]
While it is never clear what such freedom means, it is
quite evident that the rhetoric intends from an arbitrary

moment of authority which, following Newman, Perelman
and Booth, generates an accumulative momentum that
demands an inescapable assent in a communal act of
agreement on the basis of a divine disclosure which has
never taken place (Klemm admits the death of the God of
theism) except within the unavoidable, because finally
inarguable, claims of the rhetoric of persuasion.

The point is that the rhetoric demands a consensus,
while argumentation settles matters only when the audience to which it is addressed arrive at that same
consensus on the issue argued: a neat circle. The rhetoric
of theological argument: 'and, sure, he is an honourable
man'.

> I speak not to disprove what Brutus spoke,
> But here I am to speak what I do know.

That, of course, cannot be denied.

The New Rhetoric, or rather the new defence of rhetoric in Perelman and Klemm, not to speak of the very
different, profoundly conservative, defence offered by
Professor Brian Vickers in his massive study *In Defence of
Rhetoric* (1988), rejects uncompromisingly the discourse
and insights of so-called postmodernity in either its
deconstructive, nihilistic or potentially constructive
phases. Generally in postmodernity, suggests Vickers,
'rhetoric is fragmented and then subordinated to an alien
enterprise'.[24] I suspect Vickers' critique, particularly of
the writings of Paul de Man, not simply because of its
(deliberate?) misreadings, but because it claims to be
taking an authoritative stance outside the notion of rhetoric
itself. I hope it is clear by now from what I have argued
and also my manner of discourse, that I do not believe
this to be possible or legitimate. Where rhetoric confronts
it will move towards a consummation, a consumption of
its willing victims, for is there no reason in its saying, and
we are not wood, we are not stones, but men. We are,

indeed, willing to be persuaded. Like Kenneth Burke in *The Rhetoric of Religion* (1961) we readily and eagerly move from arguments to communal myths of assent, and the dark power of rhetoric, the Night-mare Life-in-Death,[25] has won again.

It is precisely this nightmare that postmodernity has sought to expose, but with its own rhetoric whose hermeneutic of suspicion is characterised not by confrontation but, like Freud, by the reverse.

Let me begin to explain what I mean by a brief reference to the work of the French thinker Jean Baudrillard. In *Simulacra and Simulations* (1981), Baudrillard develops a theory of commodity culture in which no code has priority over the consumer object and our lives are embedded in a world of images which have no referent or ground in any 'reality' except their own – a purely rhetorical world.[26] Deeply pessimistic, Baudrillard envisages consummation in terms of an engagement in a pure consumerism – a nihilistic running down the road in the self-destructive realisation of what is only our nature. Only thus can the crass rhetoric of simulacra be 'bottomed out'. As he puts it:

> a system is abolished only by pushing it into hyperlogic, by forcing it into an excessive practice which is equivalent to a brutal amortalization. 'You want us to consume – OK, let's consume always more, and anything whatsoever; for any useless and absurd purpose'.[27]

Though identified by Gianni Vattimo as 'an accomplished nihilism (which) calls us to a fictionalised experience which is also our only possibility for freedom',[28] Baudrillard, it seems to me, with fundamentalist religious zeal, presses home a self-consuming rhetoric which, like all good rhetoric, defeats argument in a relentless, inescapable drive to a communal assent – an education in corruption in which the divine and its complete negation are one and the same. Baudrillard follows the pattern of all fundamentalist rhetoric, his style being hyperbolic and declarative, often failing in sustained analysis, totalising and without limits set to its claims.

Like the even nastier eroticism of Georges Bataille, Baudrillard's writing is a rhetoric of theological argument in reverse, viewed, as it were, from behind. Chillingly, the rhetoric is one and the same in its formal conceit, for morally it does not matter, in the end, which side you come out on. Either way you are trapped in an assent to power without limit in the circle of formalism. In the Preface to *Madame Edwarda*, Bataille explains his 'primary theological attitude', perversely:

> God is nothing if He is not, in every sense, the surpassing of God: in the sense of common everyday being, in the sense of dread, horror and impurity, and, finally, in the sense of nothing . . . We cannot with impunity incorporate the very word into our speech which surpasses words, the word *God*; directly we do so this word, surpassing itself, explodes past its defining, restrictive limits. That which the word is, stops nowhere, is checked by nothing, it is everything and, everywhere, is impossible to overtake anywhere. And he who so much as suspects this instantly falls silent. Or, hunting for a way out, and realizing that he seals himself all the more inextricably into the impasse, he searches within himself for that which, capable of annihilating him, renders him similar to God, similar to nothing.[29]

Once again the linguistic and rhetorical impasse, for always within the circle one cannot get to the side of rhetoric, which is the impasse also, though reversed, of Perelman and Klemm. Only the violence in Bataille, as in Foucault, recognises more brutally the implications of the fact that as Hugo Meynell nervously admits in a recent essay on Foucault, 'the existence and implementation of power

within human society is inevitable'.[30] For Bataille, this
power, which is violence, exists permanently within a
rhetoric in which the daring of language invites the inversion of its own order and claims, like Mark Antony,
much reason where there is no ideal, no code – though
the plebians know that there's not a nobler man in Rome
than Antony . . . or so they are persuaded.

More acutely, and ultimately perhaps more tragically,
than either Bataille, Foucault or Baudrillard, the postmodernism of Jacques Derrida recognises that no language
free from all rhetoric is possible:[31] that in the *aporia*, or
impassable passage of his realm of rhetoric, the language
which expresses deconstructive processes within textuality
itself betrays the insights of that powerful centre 'Derrida'
himself – and no-one perceives this more readily than
Derrida himself, though not without irony.

It is Habermas, in his devastating study *The Philosophical Discourse of Modernity* (1985), who has exposed
most powerfully, with his own rhetoric, how 'Derrida
wants to expand the sovereignty of rhetoric over the
realm of the logical in order to solve the problem con-
fronting the totalising critique of reason.'[32] Habermas
suggests that Derrida is particularly interested in standing the primacy of logic over rhetoric, canonised since
Aristotle, on its head,[33] subordinating philosophy to
literature (or, more precisely, literary criticism) and,
recognising that there is no escape from rhetoric, striving,
it seems, for a purity of rhetorical play which finally
recognises its own self-referentiality.

Such purity is, of course, unobtainable, and it is note-
worthy how frequently the notion of 'original sin' – in
Immanuel Levinas the guilt which is 'pre-original'[34] –
occurs in Derrida's writing.

Derrida's procedures are, crucially, 'literary'. He pro-
ceeds, in Habermas' words, 'by a critique of style, in that
he finds something like indirect communications, by
which the text itself denies its manifest content, in the

rhetorical surplus of meaning inherent in the literary strata of texts that present themselves as non-literary'.[35] In particular, we may say, Derrida compels texts by Husserl, Saussure, or Rousseau to confess their guilt – the inescapable guilt of rhetoric.

Against this raging tiger of guilt, Derrida sets, and exposes the false knowledge and security of what he describes as the 'Greek element' in the Western tradition. He begins his paper 'Violence and Metaphysics. An Essay on the Thought of Immanuel Levinas'[36] with a reference to Matthew Arnold's distinction between Hebraism and Hellenism in *Culture and Anarchy* (1869) and there expands on a comparison made by Levinas, in an essay entitled 'The Trace of the Other', between Ulysses and Abraham:

> To the myth of Ulysses returning to Ithaca, we would prefer to oppose the story of Abraham leaving his country for ever for an as yet unknown land, and forbidding his servant to take back even his son to the point of departure.[37]

If the Greek hero returns home to know it properly for the first time, the Jewish patriarch is a wanderer who does not look back, who strides away from the aporia of an ever-returning rhetoric. Such brave exploration would seem to fulfil Levinas' desire, as Derrida puts it, for a language which 'would be purified of all rhetoric',[38] purified of the self-reflexive formalism of the scene of persuasion; but would such a language still deserve its name? Would it not, as it ceases to have point, simply transform its knowledge into power, which is capable of inflicting violence unseen, as it were, from behind. Is that the insight of Kafka in whose story 'In the Penal Colony', the prisoners have their crimes inscribed upon their backs – become themselves the texts of their offences?

Many questions were troubling the explorer, but at the sight of the prisoner he asked only: 'Does he know his sentence?' 'No', said the officer, eager to go on with his exposition, but the explorer interrupted him: 'He doesn't know the sentence that has been passed on him?' 'No', said the officer, again pausing a moment as if to let the explorer elaborate his question, and then said: 'There would be no point in telling him. He'll learn it on his body.'[39]

Into the back-door of this prison-house, Abraham tramps wearily, a stranger in a land of infinitely-receding promise. In Levinas' world of a language which is never free from rhetoric but which, like Abraham's people, exists permanently on the edge of a state of collapse beyond which there is the eternal possibility of an experience freed from division and constraints of system,[40] 'God alone', in Derrida's words, 'keeps (the) world from being a world of the pure and worst violence, a world of immorality itself'. He continues:

The structures of living and naked experience described by Levinas are the very structures of a world in which war would rage – strange conditional – if the infinitely other were not infinity, if there were, by chance, one naked man, finite and alone. But in this case, Levinas would no doubt say, there no longer would be any war, for there would be neither face nor true asymmetry. Therefore the naked and living experience in which God has *already* begun to speak could no longer be our concern. In other words, in a world where the face would be fully respected (as that which is not of this world), there no longer would be war. In a world where the face would no longer be absolutely respected, where there no longer would be a face, there would be no more cause for a war. God, therefore, is implicated in war. His name too, like the name of peace, is a function within the system of war, the only system whose basis permits us to speak, the only system whose language may ever be spoken. With or without God, there would be no war. War supposes and exludes God. We can have a relation to God only within such a system.[41]

In a world where there is no longer a face, without confrontation of theological persuasion, Levinas' inevitable rhetoric of postmodernity perceives the divine presence as in the promise of Exodus 33: 20–3, wherein no man shall see God and live: 'my face shall not be seen'. In the a-theology of the postmodern, in Derrida and Levinas, is revealed a rhetoric of reversal, the opposite of the Hellenistic Perelman, Booth or Klemm, and which, like Freud and his Wolf-Man, wants to use us from behind, with suspicion. In fact, it seems to me, what the new theological interest in rhetoric has tended to expose is, on the one hand, the power games of the Christian tradition upon which David Klemm, like Newman before him, is drawing, and the terrifying anti-semitic tendencies in vast areas of post-enlightenment thought, from the hermeneutics of suspicion of Freud and Nietzsche, which postmodernist writings have, by implication, suggested. Hence the perplexing nervousness of Jewish thinkers like Derrida and Levinas who feel deeply the threat in the aporia of their own arguments.

And, to ask a question which continues to reverberate in different ways throughout these reflections, is there a way out, or must all theological or a-theological rhetoric finally be practised 'in camera', in the vicious closed systems of a self-defining formalism? A brief, inadequate note, in conclusion to this chapter without conclusion, and dependent, as Coleridge would say, on fugitive causes.

No-one knows better than Derrida himself the truncated nature of the rhetoric which he employs,[42] with only three of the five parts of the classical theory of persuasive discourse, lacking the 'voice' of *elocutio* and *actio*. But within the profoundly conservative circle of Derrida's rhetoric is glimpsed an instance of prioritising which Klemm's rhetoric of theological argument finally eliminates. For if, in the four master tropes, David Klemm identifies synedoche as marking the inbreaking of God from outside the linguistic structure, in Derrida's theory of the trace, which derives from Freud's general model for perception and memory (ironically, given the opening remarks on Freud in this chapter), is celebrated the tropic moment of irony as the moment of strategic in-breaking,[43] as the presence or trace of absence as disturbing alterity.

Derrida's complex theory of the trace, worked out in his general theory of Writing, is restated, with consummate irony, by Levinas in his essay 'The Trace of the Other' in a revised reading of Exodus 33. Perhaps the ironic is the 'true' reading of that Exodus passage wherein, in Levinas' words, 'the God who passed is not the model of which the face would be an image'.[44] Here, in other words, is not merely the reversal of the rhetoric of confrontation, but an ironic turn on the words – not the other which is wholly other, but the presence of an absence in the trace in a different word-play. In such deep play in language, may be traced a potential restoration of values in argumentation or dispute – unlike the New Rhetoric's claim for a 'valid' way of distinguishing a 'good' argument from a 'bad' one – or of resolving the problem of what Lyotard calls the 'differend', that 'a universal rule of judgement between heterogeneous genres is lacking in general'.[45]

In deep play, irony and satire, however, is rhetoric simply employed to outflank the outrageous claims of rhetoric? – as if such a universal rule of judgement was conceivable! How seriously can we take the notion of *stability* in Wayne Booth's proposal for the Supreme Ironist, or does this once again merely close the rhetorical circle?[46] A sharper irony, which is supremely deconstructive of its own rhetoric (is it irony or not?) is noted by D.J. Enright in Samuel Butler's brilliant *Erewhon*

(1872) whose hero remarks: 'Once I had to leap down a not inconsiderable waterfall into a deep pool below, and my swag was so heavy that I very nearly drowned. I had indeed a hairbreadth escape; but, as luck would have it, Providence was on my side'. Enright remarks:

> Only those aware of an ancient distinction between capital-P Providence and luck will perceive the joke, the satirical dig at the Church. For most younger readers today, I imagine, the statement must appear merely tautologous, a defect of style, as if to say 'luckily I was lucky'. Butler might be thought to have been hoist with his own petard. It is a risk all verbal engineers run.[47]

And the reader, in her turn, must remain wary, on guard.

Notes

1. See, Stanley Fish, *Doing What Comes Naturally* pp. 471–2.
2. Donald N. McCloskey, *The Rhetoric of Economics* (Wisconsin, 1985) pp. 28–9, 47.
3. Fish, op. cit. p. 486.
4. Stanley Fish, 'Withholding the missing portion: power, meaning and persuasion in Freud's *The Wolf Man*' in Fabb, Attridge, Durant and MacCabe (Eds.), *The Linguistics of Writing* p. 156.
5. Fish, ibid. p. 169.
6. Richard Rorty, *Consequences of Pragmatism* (Minneapolis, 1982) p. 92.
7. Mark C. Taylor, *Altarity* (Chicago and London, 1987) p. 211.
8. Chaim Perelman, *The New Rhetoric and the Humanities* (Dordrecht, 1979) p. 10.
9. Ibid. p. 7.
10. Carroll C. Arnold, Introduction to the *Realm of Rhetoric* p. xvi.
11. Perelman, *The Realm of Rhetoric*, p. 159.
12. Ibid.
13. See, J.H. Newman, *The Grammar of Assent* (1870).
14. Newman, quoted in John Coulson, *Religion and Imagination* (Oxford, 1981) p. 58.
15. Newman, quoted in Bernard Lonergan, *Method in Theology* (London, 1972) p. 388.
16. Wayne C. Booth, *Modern Dogma and the Rhetoric of Assent* p. 197.
17. S.T. Coleridge, *Biographia Literaria* (1817). Collected Coleridge Vol. 7. Ed. James Engell and W. Jackson Bate (Princeton, 1983) p. 9.

18. Shakespeare, *Julius Caesar* III. 2. 106–8.
19. See, Nelson, Megill, and McCloskey, *The Rhetoric of the Human Sciences* (Wisconsin, 1987) pp. 276–97; *Journal of the American Academy of Religion* LV (1987) 443–69; *Literature and Theology* III (1989), 267–84.
20. Klemm, 'The Rhetoric of Theological Argument'. Nelson, Megill, McCloskey, p. 278. See also above Chapter 6, pp. 95–6.
21. Ibid. p. 280.
22. Klemm, 'Toward a Rhetoric of Postmodern Theology', p. 447.
23. Klemm, 'Ricoeur, Theology and the Rhetoric of Overturning'. *Literature and Theology* III (1989) 281.
24. Brian Vickers, *In Defence of Rhetoric* (Oxford, 1988) p. 447.
25. See, S.T.C. Coleridge, 'The Rime of the Ancient Mariner', line 193.
26. See also, Jean Baudrillard, *Selected Writings* (Oxford, 1989) pp. 5–6.
27. Baudrillard, *In the Shadow of the Silent Minorities* (New York, 1983) p. 46.
28. Gianni Vattimo, *The End of Modernity* Trans. John R. Snyder. (Oxford, 1988) p. 29.
29. Georges Bataille, Preface to *Madame Edwarda*. p. 142.
30. Hugo Meynell, 'On Knowledge, Power and Michel Foucault'. *The Heythrop Journal* XXX (1989) 431.
31. Jacques Derrida, *Writing and Difference* (London 1978) p. 147.
32. Jürgen Habermas, *The Philosophical Discourse of Modernity* (Oxford, 1987; first publ. 1985) p. 188.
33. Ibid. pp. 187–210.
34. See, Mark Taylor, op. cit. p. 211.
35. Habermas, op. cit. p. 189.
36. Derrida, op. cit. pp. 79–153.
37. Levinas 'La Trace de L'autre', quoted in Derrida, op. cit. p. 320.
38. Derrida, ibid. p. 147.
39. Franz Kafka, *Penal Colony: Stories and Short Pieces* (New York, 1961) p. 197.
40. See, Bataille, *My Mother, Madame Edwarda, The Dead Man* Trans. Austryn Wainhouse (London, New York, 1989) p. 214.
41. Derrida, op. cit. p. 107.
42. See, Stephen Tyler, *The Unspeakable: Discourse, Dialogue and Rhetoric in the Postmodern World* (Wisconsin, 1987) pp. 46–7.
43. See, Richard Harland, *Superstructuralism* (London, 1987) pp. 143 ff.
44. E. Levinas, 'The Trace of the Other', in Mark C. Taylor, Ed. *Deconstruction in Context* (Chicago, 1986) p. 359.
45. Jean-François Lyotard, *The Differend: Phases in Dispute*. Trans. Georges Van Den Abbeele (Manchester, 1988) p. xi.
46. Wayne C. Booth, *The Rhetoric of Irony* pp. 268–9. See also above chapter 4, pp. 60–1.
47. D.J. Enright, *The Alluring Problem* pp. 61–2.

8

Postmodernism, Rhetoric and Irony: Another Modest Proposal

There is a celebrated conversation between the novelist George Eliot and F.W.H. Myers which took place in Cambridge in 1873. Myers records it rhapsodically:

> I remember how, at Cambridge, I walked with her once in the Fellows' Garden of Trinity, on an evening of rainy May; and she, stirred somewhat beyond her wont, and taking as her text the three words which have been used so often as the inspiring trumpet calls of men, – the words *God*, *Immortality*, *Duty*, – pronounced, with terrible earnestness, how inconceivable was the *first*, how unbelievable the *second*, and yet how peremptory and absolute the *third*. Never, perhaps have sterner accents affirmed the sovereignty of impersonal and unrecompensing Law. I listened and night fell; her grave, majestic countenance turned towards me like a Sibyl's in the gloom; it was as though she withdrew from my grasp, one by one, the two scrolls of promise, and left me the third scroll only, awful with inevitable fates. And when we stood at length and parted, amid that columnar circuit of the forest-trees, between the last twilight of starless skies, I seemed to be gazing like Titus at Jerusalem, on vacant seats and empty halls, – on a sanctuary with no Presence to hallow it, and heaven left lonely of a God.[1]

Although often quoted as a description of mid-Victorian religious doubt, Myers' account sounds a peculiarly contemporary note in our postmodern world with its sense of lost Presence, abandonment of the metaphysical tradition and arguments against 'logocentrism'. Against postmodernism, George Steiner has recently denied claims for the death of God and argues that 'the experience of aesthetic meaning in particular, that of literature, of the arts, of musical form, infers the necessary possibilities of this 'real presence'.[2] The adoption by Steiner of the religious language of sacrament in the context of literature may be reversed as Myers' profoundly agnostic sense of duty in a godless world is shifted to the religious context in which the celebration of the sacrament is 'our duty and our joy'.[3] And if duty exists only in a world not under unrecompensing law, but under grace, then we might do well to consider at this stage, and in addition, Friedrich Schlegel's affirmation that 'Irony is duty'.[4]

Duty implies commitment and responsibility. For Myers, the disappearance of God in the nineteenth century left only the stern demands of a high Victorian moral humanism, a religion of humanity. As we have seen, throughout the Christian tradition and in various ways there has existed a close rhetorical relationship between the church community and its sacred texts, which may either be scriptual, or liturgical – books of prayer, divine office or forms of the sacraments – or doctrinal – the creeds or statements of great councils like Chalcedon in 451 AD. In his suspicion of textual artifice in the *Phaedrus* and the *Seventh Letter* Plato was acutely aware of the inherent fragility of writing, and the ambiguous relationship with truth of the strong textual call to communal duty. Under the guise of ignorance and learning from others, Socrates practised his teaching of others. St Paul, or so he assures us, thought a great deal of those who seemed to be ignorant and foolish, although he does not show many signs of actually regarding himself as amongst their number.

In their texts, societies and communities tell the stories which form their traditions, an exercise clearly at work in the New Testament narratives of the four gospels and the Acts of the Apostles. Brian Stock, in his recent book *Listening for the Text* (1989), has commented that:

> Societies may tell different stories, but when we come to retell them, we use a limited range of explanatory and persuasive techniques. History used to be a branch of rhetoric. If we wish to understand what is said in old or new social narratives, literary analysis is still essential. For there are no tales without implied narrators and audiences: the social function of texts, as well as the literary function of societies, consists of maintaining the metaphysical links. What is more, stories do not convince us by their arguments, but by their lifelikeness. They may be verifiable, if we can get at the 'facts'; but mainly they are believable.[5]

Adherence to the 'stories' of the religious communities' central texts is a fundamental duty, since they represent and embody in the formulations of theological doctrine the essential continuity, the apostolicity, which guarantees the community's identity. And if history, as a crucial element in Christian theology, is a branch of rhetoric, so the guiding texts, it may be said, function rhetorically, not by their arguments, but by their 'lifelikeness', or, in other words, their ability to persuade us that they are 'true' and to create in us a disposition to act in a particular way. Any rhetorical means will justify its end.

Through its texts, the religious community is bounden in its duty to what is perceived as the truth, and by the sacred text, we may be sure, we are led into all truth. The implication of such a sense of duty is that there are essences – essential truths – to discover or perceive, and that some idea or referent outside language guarantees its ultimate stability. Theology and philosophy together, therefore, are dutifully engaged in the pursuit of truth, and the one or the other will exercise a powerful domination. However, thinkers like Derrida and other postmoderns (and post-modernism has actually existed throughout the history of textuality) would question whether such determination of the point of human existence is desirable or even available. Truth, if it exists, is not discovered but created within the changing contingencies of experience; language is not stable or inherently referential, but unstable, living and pragmatically adaptable, specific to the moment.[6] Derrida in 'The White Mythology' usefully quotes from Anatole France's 'Garden of Epicurus' to illustrate the enervating effect of theologians and 'metaphysicians' who claim an approach to universality in their linguistic programmes.

> . . . the metaphysicians, when they make up a new language are like knife-grinders, who grind coins and medals against their stone instead of knives and scissors. They rub out the relief, the inscriptions, the portraits, and when one can no longer see on the coins Victoria, or Wilhelm, or the French Republic, they explain: these coins now have nothing specifically English or German or French about them, for we have taken them out of time and space; they are now no longer worth, say, five francs, but rather have an inestimable value, and the area in which they are a medium of exchange has been infinitely extended.[7]

So we may dare to speak with the whole company of earth and heaven, and of all ages. But despite the defences of rhetoric, and its consistent embodiment in Christian doctrine and liturgy, Plato's suspicion remains that the skills and techniques of language employed by communities in the maintenance of their textual identity have only a fragile relationship with the virtue and truth which they claim: in the business of persuasion they quietly accede to the end justifying the means. Flattery, threat, easy promise are never far distant. In his letters to the Philippians, Colossians and I Thessalonians, St Paul opens with words that soothe and flatter: some might call it buttering your audience up.

We have seen how Stanley Fish demonstrates the formalism of rhetoric – its unavoidable, inescapable nature within discourse.[8] And if Aristotle seeks to defend rhetoric as the partner of logic and reason, the very formalism of its procedures reinforces the assumptions that make one suspicious – that there exists an independent reality which can be observed in its essence by clear thinking, and then represented in a transparent verbal medium.[9] Insofar as rhetoric creates a powerful disposition to believe that such is the case, so theology or philosophy is confirmed in its object of pursuing and defining the truth. The circle is neatly closed.

Professor Steiner confesses that the logic of the postmodernism which actually admits such circularity in itself is irrefutable. Quite simply, it instructs us that 'nothing shall come of nothing'.[10] What Steiner refuses to admit is that the claims of deconstruction embrace rhetorically also that which has been deconstructed. They cannot be right in their own terms without also being right in their exposure of the duplicity of the logocentric tradition of Western tradition. That is the point that Fish is making.

But what, then, of the possibility of a spirituality? Or, in the other terms, have the imaginative claims of literature or the revelatory claims of the Judaeo–Christian tradition simply melted in air, into thin air?

> Yea, all which it inherit, shall dissolve
>
> And like this insubstantial pageant faded,
> Leave not a rack behind.[11]

One thing, I think, is clear. We cannot with Steiner, turn the clock back, or else, like him, we will find ourselves hoist on the petard of our own romantic rhetoric, inheritors of a heaven left lonely of a God.

What, then, of our other duty which is ironic? It is, if nothing else, profoundly poetic for, as Richard Rorty has put it, 'the generic task of the ironist is the one Coleridge recommended to the great and original poet: to create the taste by which he will be judged'.[12] Irony, to counter Fish's words on persuasion, is precisely the business of catching oneself in the act, so that one becomes freed from the metaphysical urge and the obsession with theory. Ironically, as Paul de Man perceived, it is a theoretical resistance to the theoretical enterprise itself, which never attempts to rub out the contingent, particular inscriptions or portraits on the discourse which is our daily, local currency in conversation – those things which make us real and individual. Irony is never satisfying in itself, and arises out of the peculiar requirements of each situation.[13] This has nothing to do with any notion of 'stable irony'.[14] Endlessly self-reflexive, irony engages in a perpetual redescription of established beliefs and assumptions in order to break free from their power. Its centre of activity is always other than its ostensible theme, so that one of the great ironic documents in the English language is S.T. Coleridge's *Biographia Literaria* (1817) which, purporting to be an intellectual history through philosophers like Descartes, Kant, Schelling and Fichte and poets like Wordsworth, is actually a series of self-reflexive vignettes of the moment of thought, a self-critical reflection on the process of reading as a point of reference for critical procedures. *Biographia Literaria* in discussing Kant is not *about* Kant. Its difficulty and inspiration lies in what Fish calls 'progressive decertainising', 'purposeful disorientation' or 'expectations of clarity thwarted'.[15] It is a freedom from system, but it is nothing if not uncomfortable. To be serious enough to see the joke has not been a notable Christian virtue – to perceive, for example, the irony lurking in the parable of the unjust (but remarkably shrewd) steward in Luke 16: 1–9. Not untypically, J.F. Powers' Father Urban found the parable problematic and likely to do more harm than good, and suggested that Jesus was perhaps a little tired when he first told it.[16] Actually, the irony is energetic when the tension is most extreme between the surface discourse and the deep structure of the text, when what is said is closest to its own opposite. That is why Nietzsche's *Twilight of the Idols (or, How to Philosophize with a Hammer)* (1889) is paradigmatically ironic in its recognition that something fundamental in Western identity and destiny – history, metaphysics – has run its course. Everything now must be remade.[17] Nietzsche offers the maxim:

> Help thyself: then everyone will help thee too. Principle of Christian charity.[18]

It is irony worthy of Jesus himself; a text within a text deconstructively meeting its opposite. We may compare the gospel saying, 'He who would save his life, must lose it' (Luke 17: 33).

I suggest we might call this ironic redescription or remaking the principle of *intratextuality,* as opposed to the now more familiar idea of intertextuality which we have learnt from Julia Kristeva and others. The term *intratextual* is first used, as far as I am aware, though in a more general sense than I am intending here, by George Lindbeck in his book *The Nature of Doctrine* (1984). Lindbeck describes the intratextual task as 'a matter of explicating [texts'] contents and the perspectives on extra-textual reality that they generate'. I am more concerned with the literary question of how texts inhabit each other, refracting their textuality between the layers of their artistry. In *Hamlet* much is made of the play within the play, by which Hamlet intends to expose Claudius through the pricking of his conscience:

> the play's the thing
> Wherein I'll catch the conscience of the King.

> (*Hamlet*. II. 2. 609)

Nathan the prophet had used a similar device to catch the conscience of King David (2 Samuel 12: 1–15), another text within the text. As Hamlet lays his plans with the players he uses the phrase employed by Richard Rorty in the title of his book *Philosophy and the Mirror of Nature* (1980):

> Be not too tame neither, but let your own discretion be your tutor, suit the action to the word, the word to the action, with this special observance, that you o'erstep not the modesty of nature; for any thing so o'erdone is from the purpose of playing, whose end both at the first, and now, was and is, to hold as 'twere the mirror up to nature, to show virtue her own feature, scorn her own image, and the very age and body of the time his form and pressure . . .

> (III. 2.)

There is irony at work here. For Rorty uses the phrase against his contention that philosophy should be a 'mirroring' of some assumed reality or essence. It is precisely this by which Hamlet hopes to confront Claudius with the image of himself, a mirror inescapably held up for his conscience to scrutinise.

Hamlet, it would seem, is using an artistic device which Rorty, in his anti-essentialism, in his philosophy denies. But, the point of the device in *Hamlet* is that it is a play within a play, a text within a text. Not reality itself, or even a claim to reality, but the achievement of what Coleridge recognised as the generic task of the ironist: the creation of that by which judgement is made, a fulcrum upon which the conscience is momentarily caught in the uneasy, fleeting moment of play. In that moment, that which is becomes its own opposite, and Claudius stares himself in the face.

Not the text, but the text within the text: intratextuality. Irony, inherently unstable and destabilising, happily works against its own narrative discourse and against its own textuality. The best irony is barely perceptible, almost possessed by its reader but finally eluding the constructive possibilities of the power inherent in accepted canonicity. In Laurence Sterne's *The Life and Opinions of Tristram Shandy* (1759–67) it is suggested that:

> It is the nature of a hypothesis, when once a man has conceived it, that it assimilates every thing to itself, as proper nourishment; and, from the first moment of your begetting it, it generally grows the stronger by everything you see, hear, read, or understand. This is of great use.[20]

No doubt of immediate encouragement to the average biblical critic, the truth of the remark will be appreciated by all theorists: until, enthusiasm starting to wane, the suspicion enters that you are beginning to miss the point. But by then it is too late. The text within the text speaks uncomfortably but all too often ineffectually against the powerful rhetoric of the initial proposal – thus orthodoxy casts its spell. It becomes our duty to believe it, or we can no longer afford not to.

Allow me to offer, therefore, a further modest proposal in suitably bad theological taste but as an antidote to the formalism of language and 'serious' rhetoric. I refer back, of course, to Jonathan Swift's impeccable *A Modest Proposal, for preventing the children of the poor people from being a burden to their parents or country, and for making them beneficial to the public* (1729). We know, of course, that rhetoric is merely a necessary instrument of deception to achieve a greater end, and that, as Swift told Pope, man is not truly a rational animal, but an animal capable of reasoning. A perfectly reasonable argument may therefore be employed to create a disposition to adhere to any premise – the end will justify any means (and the just will happily live by faith). Swift is an excellent rhetorician:

I think it is agreed by all parties that this prodigious number of children, in the arms, or on the backs, or at the heels of their mothers, and frequently of their fathers, is in the present deplorable state of the kingdom a very great additional grievance; and therefore whoever could find out a fair, cheap and easy method of making these children sound useful members of the commonwealth would deserve so well of the public as to have his statue set up for a preserver of the nation.[21]

The suggestion that poor Irish infants be utilised as comestibles is eminently reasonable: the alternatives are a life of crime or to become cannon-fodder in battle; simple arithmetic speaks in its defence, and the eating is good. Economics are satisfied, not to speak of morality, since such a policy is an inducement to marriage and the proper care of children – the fatter the baby, the better the eating. In conclusion, Swift emphasises that he has absolutely no vested interests in the proposal himself since his wife is past child-bearing age and his own children grown up and therefore presumably too tough.

A perfect argument, and a warning to all perfect arguments when the stakes are high! Swift was entirely serious, though we might say that his humour was in bad taste. But when, as has been recently suggested,[22] good taste and humour are a contradiction in terms, 'like a chaste whore', we might be forgiven for thinking that the ground beneath our feet is becoming very shaky, whores being professionally chased without being remotely chaste. On the other hand, our Lord spoils the argument in this particular matter by suggesting of one member of that ancient profession that those who are forgiven most will love their forgiver most. The irony is so obvious that it is extraordinary how often we miss the point 'in real life'.

The text within the text of *A Modest Proposal* is powerful enough. Any sensible reader would know that the

Irish children would not actually be eaten. My further modest proposal treads even more dangerous ground, partly because it is from scripture, and because, for that reason, we happily hear the word and assume its power, refusing to acknowledge the intratext, that unstable redescription within which is broken the rhetoric of the tradition and the spell cast by reading the books which make up its canon. We read in St Matthew's Gospel that:

> The kingdom of heaven is like treasure hidden in a field which a man found and covered up; then in his joy he goes and sells all that he has and buys that field.
> (13: 44)

Robert Scharlemann, in his essay entitled 'Being "as Not". Overturning the Ontological',[23] dissects the irony of those familiar words, although he is perhaps a bit too serious himself to perceive it as ironic.

There are the standard, Christian writers on the parables, and they all assume that the parables of the kingdom, if not allegories, are still metaphors, and that, as Ricoeur puts it, 'metaphor is the rhetorical process by which discourse unleashes the power that certain fictions have to redescribe reality'.[24] Once again we find ourselves slipping our heads into the rhetorical and mimetic noose. On the whole, its products in the Christian tradition have been unedifying – not as bad, perhaps, as chewing on infant limbs, but nearly as dishonest in their claims to truth and the power that goes with them. The choice ends up as believe, or be damned.

But in the phrase 'the kingdom of heaven' the sense of being and not being are closely intertwined.[25] For to speak of the kingdom of heaven is to speak of a kingdom that does not exist like any kingdom which grants that word referential qualities. It is a kingdom that, ironically, is not a kingdom at all. The phrase, as Scharlemann puts it, is the combination of a *denominator* (kingdom) and an *alienator* (heaven), of a kingdom which is alienated from itself. There is a text within a text, that, in short, 'the kingdom of heaven is the kingdom of heaven as what is not the kingdom of heaven'.[26] The parable, in other words, like all irony, is inherently unstable and destabilising, performing a disjunctive act between its ontological promise (that we may find out something, if only by analogy, about heaven) and its theological overturning. Unlike the case of Swift, the bad taste lies not in the apparent promise, but in its ironic overturning. With some *relief* we realise that we are not being invited to consume our infants: with *anger* and *consternation* we begin to suspect that we are not being offered the cosy comfort of heaven in ordinary.

The trouble is that the tradition in the Christian community has usually failed to realise this, and too often paid the penalty, its deep unease demonstrated in theological circles in that, although we are pretty certain that we have things sized up, we feel that we had better write one more 'definitive' commentary on the Bible, or one more 'systematic' theology, just in case. Power must be maintained, and authority reaffirmed. The church which has refrained from consuming infants has often, nevertheless, demonstrated its bad taste by burning its opponents, or, at the very least, their books.

I am not, therefore, inclined to apologise for my parabolic bad taste. The parable, which *apparently* likens the kingdom of heaven to the event of a man buying a field, by its combination of denominator and alienator, suggests merely that the kingdom of heaven *is* the occurrence *when* the kingdom of heaven is *not* being the kingdom of heaven. To be a citizen of such a kingdom demands living with heavy irony and a recognition of an absolute self-reflexivity which is prepared to face its own opposite fair and square. It is that self-redescription which Augustine has to come to terms with in the *Confessions*, forced to it by the supreme ironist, God:

But while he was speaking, O Lord, you were turning me around to look at myself. For I had placed myself behind my own back, refusing to see myself.[27]

But the supreme ironist who is, in Augustine's words, 'forcing me upon my own sight', is not Wayne Booth's stable ironist who continues to claim stability in values and truth. We need to beware of such a deity, a god of those who fear freedom and the familiar god of Dostoyevsky's Grand Inquisitor. He is the rhetorician whom Socrates feared, the fragile fixity of his written word being an obstacle in the path of wisdom.

Irony is unstable and, in the first instance, private, a text deep within public textuality. The gloomy French diarist and critic, Henri-Frédéric Amiel (1821–81) remarked that 'Not to take yourself seriously is an affront to God'. But to take yourself too seriously is far worse and in the worst possible taste. Such an offence is best countered with an innoculation of irony, a needle of bad taste to set us right again and at least remind ourselves that we are rhetoricians for whom truth, goodness and beauty are 'artifacts whose fundamental design we often have to alter'.[28] Then we may be less susceptible to that profoundly Christian art of missing the joke and become more prepared to risk the bet that it *might* be true in a larger sense. As Robert Detweiler puts it in an essay on 'Jesus jokes':

> The laughter is crucial. It can signal a welcome to chaos' rule, or it can mean the dismay of recognition, the insight into the self that impels us to change. If laughing at Jesus means this last, a laughing at ourselves that provokes and accompanies *metanoia*, then we can proclaim his life and death as a grand joke indeed.[29]

And if the joke is painful to our delicate religious sensibility, then at least we have privately felt a little of that which is alone and ultimately universal in human experience – pain and humiliation. We have, then, something to share, a duty to bear together, a reminder of glory.

Notes

1. F.W.H. Myers, *Essays – Modern* (London, 1883) pp. 268–9.
2. George Steiner, *Real Presences* (London, 1989) p. 3.
3. E.g., The Eucharistic Prayer on p. 130 of *The Alternative Service Book* of the Church of England (1980).
4. Quoted in D.J. Enright, *The Alluring Problem*, p. 18.
5. Brian Stock, *Listening for the Text* (Baltimore and London, 1989) pp. 10–11.
6. See, Richard Rorty, *Philosophy and the Mirror of Nature* (Oxford, 1989), Chap. VIII: 'Philosophy Without Mirrors'. *Contingency, Irony, and Solidarity* (Cambridge, 1989), Chap. I: 'The contingency of language'.
7. Anatole France, quoted in Rorty, *Philosophy and the Mirror of Nature* p. 368.
8. Stanley Fish, 'Withholding the missing portion: power, meaning and persuasion in Freud's *The Wolf-Man*' p. 170. See also above, Chapter 7, pp. 105–6.
9. See, Stanley Fish, *Doing What Comes Naturally*, p. 478–9.
10. George Steiner, 'Real Presences'. The Leslie Stephen Memorial Lecture (Cambridge, 1986) p. 23.
11. Shakespeare, *The Tempest*, IV. 1. 154–6.
12. Rorty, *Contingency, Irony and Solidarity*, p. 97.
13. See, William Empson, *Seven Types of Ambiguity* (London, 1984) p. 235.
14. See, Wayne C. Booth, *A Rhetoric of Irony*, Chap. 1.
15. See, Kathleen M. Wheeler, *Sources, processes and methods in Coleridge's 'Biographia Literaria'* (Cambridge, 1980) p. 158.
16. See, Enright, op. cit. p. 56.
17. See, Rorty, *Contingency, Irony and Solidarity*, p. 101.
18. F. Nietzsche, *Twilight of the Idols* (Harmondsworth, 1990) p. 33.
19. George A. Lindbeck, *The Nature of Doctrine: Religion and Theology in a Postliberal Age* (Philadelphia, 1984) p. 117.
20. See, Enright, op. cit. p. 36.
21. Jonathan Swift, *A Modest Proposal* (1729), reprinted in *The Portable Swift*, Ed. Carl Van Doren (London, 1948) p. 549.
22. By Malcolm Muggeridge.
23. In, Robert Scharlemann, *Inscriptions and Reflections. Essays in Philosophical Theology* (Charlottesville, 1989) pp. 54–65. See also above p. 10.
24. Paul Ricoeur, *The Rule of Metaphor*. Trans. Robert Czerny (Toronto, 1981) p. 7.

25. See, Scharlemann, op. cit. p. 61.
26. Ibid. p. 63.
27. St. Augustine, *Confessions*, Book VIII 7 (Harmondsworth, 1961) p. 169.
28. Richard Rorty, *Consequences of Pragmatism* (Minneapolis, 1982) p. 92.
29. Robert Detweiler, 'The Jesus Jokes: Religious Humour in the Age of Excess'. *Cross Currents*, 24 (Spring, 1974) 71.

9

The Christian Art of Missing the Joke

He's a good drum, my lord, but a naughty orator[1]

In Shakespearean comedy, the pun insistently turns words and their meaning towards what Stanley Cavell has called 'the region of the nothing',[2] between 'naught' and 'naughty'. Orators, we know, are naughty in their art of persuasion, but to be no orator is to be truly naughty in mischievous subversion of art by art itself. Shakespeare's plays are alive and grant life only in performance and become sadly desiccated as objects of classroom study and theorising. The puns and verbal wit come alive in the physical exchanges between characters whose actions promote laughter and pity and terror. The same is true in the texts of religion, which too easily become books of the Book, that is writings which are totalised by a consciousness, human or divine.[3] But the dominical command is to *action*, to do something as a memorial. Religion and its theology, like Shakespeare, needs continuously to be enacted as a counter to the totalising, enervating power politics of its sacred texts as they make their demands (in whose name?) upon submissive communities. Texts must not be allowed to forget the vigour of their textuality.

Milan Kundera suggests why the novel has been so awkward for theological discourse, and how it quickly dies when theology tries to take it over:

> Man desires a world where good and evil can be clearly distinguished, for he has an innate and irrepressible

desire to judge before he understands. Religions and ideologies are founded on this desire. They can cope with the novel only by translating its language of relativity and ambiguity into their own apodictic and dogmatic discourse. They require that someone be right . . .[4]

Great novels, especially popular novels like Jaroslav Hašek's *The Good Soldier Švejk*, which is firmly within Bakhtin's Rabelaisian tradition of literature, deconstruct by humour the terrible, structured machinery of war and institutional bureaucracy. Through the dumb isolence of Švejk, horror becomes a laughing matter and the careful articulations of power are stripped of their pretence of rational argument. As in Kafka, the aggression of force is revealed as pure irrationality. In Kundera's words:

> Kafka and Hašek . . . bring us face to face with this enormous paradox: In the course of the Modern Era, Cartesian rationality has corroded, one after the other, all the values inherited from the Middle Ages. But just when reason wins a total victory, pure irrationality (force willing only its will) seizes the world stage, because there is no longer any generally accepted value system to block its path.[5]

Like Rabelais, Hašek is vulgar and blasphemous, yet deeply creative in his destruction of authority and official culture, a major element of which are the institutions of religion whose priest readily admits, 'I represent someone who doesn't exist and myself play the part of God.'[6] But Švejk remains the Good Soldier, the playful, ironic subverter of the political rhetoric of power, undoing system and its communities. In him one is reminded of Derrida's reading of Genesis 11: 1–9, in which God is the deconstructor of the tower of Babel. 'He interrupts a construction', says Derrida. 'The deconstruction of the tower of Babel, moreover, gives a good idea what deconstruction is: an unfinished edifice whose half-completed structures are visible, letting one guess at the scaffolding behind them.'[7] In the Genesis story, the Shemites fear a loss of self-identity and engage in an act of construction, claiming universal applicability for their language. Their activity is familiar enough in communities which make religious claims and establish hierarchies of power. In Derrida's reading, God's interruption of the Shemites' constructive activities involves a linguistic fall, a 'disshemination' – and a frustration of particular structures in a particular time and place.

In what sense do modern ironists from Hasek to Derrida return us to theological possibilities? Precisely because, by possibility and ellipsis they work from within rhetoric, not with any nostalgia for its restoration, but actively doubling their way into an alternative integrity stripped of the illusions of power and metaphysics. As ironists they are, in an acute sense, interpreters and they prompt interpretation. In other words, they provoke activity and disturb assumptions, and where interpretation is made possible there also is realised the condition of impossibility for totalising a text.[8] A text then is freed to realise its textuality. The point in Derrida, of course, is analogous to Rousseau's political thesis, that 'the flaws which make social institutions necessary are the same as make the abuse of them unavoidable'.[9]

The same, indeed, will be true of the institutions of religion, which is why blasphemy is so much feared within the very necessities of belief. The sense of threat which accompanies the fear of blasphemy is a child of a totalitarian universe. It is engendered by a rhetoric which claims to reflect and promote a notion of reality and to expound a theory which accurately maps the world and its causes. The ironist, however, proposes a rhetoric which checkmates the claims of systematic rhetoric[10] and denies that the suggestion of argumentation (reason) may constitute a ground for action or conduct (cause). Thus rhetoric, with its fears and miseries, is always being undercut, and the failure of ironic writing to describe a world independent of itself is an escape from the dead hand of the mimetic – that which would offer us a vision of reality by which control may be exercised. But the claim that there is nothing outside of the text[11] is not actually formalistic: it is merely the recognition that no knowledge of which we can speak is unmediated. The act of interpretation lies at the heart of any theology, unsettled, unsettling and provoking, always resisting metaphysical illusion. Its incompatibility with the systematic tendency to totalisation is not merely political or moral, but ontological.[12] Irony, which develops from rhetoric as a figure of rhetoric, replaces a world of single Truth with ambiguity and an opaque spirit which offers texts not as mirrors to be seen through to meaning or mirrors held up to Nature, but reflexive instruments whose textuality demands relationships, and disconcerting mirrors held up to the mirror of art – the art of our philosophy, ideology and theology.[13]

Kundera identifies four appeals in the art of the novel to which he is especially responsive: the appeal of play, the appeal of dream, the appeal of thought, and the appeal of time. In each case, the novel is always threatening to break out of imperatives, of synthesis and of chronology. Its freedom from practical purpose and its fictionality render it peculiarly open to breaking down the barriers of consciousness and temporality with which the religious mind and community struggle, and it is no accident that critics like Robert Alter have elected to study biblical narratives in the manner of fiction and literary art,[14] and that rhetorical criticism in a variety of ways is increasingly fascinating students of biblical and theological texts. Kundera describes the theological and ecclesiological conditions which I have been decrying, in political terms:

The unification of the planet's history, that humanist dream which God has spitefully allowed to come true, has been accompanied by a process of dizzying reduction. True, the termites of reduction have always gnawed away at life: even the greatest love ends up as a skeleton of feeble memories. But the character of modern society hideously exacerbates this curse: it reduces man's life to its social function; the history of a people to a small set of events that are themselves reduced to a tendentious interpretation; social life is reduced to a political struggle, and that in turn to the confrontation of just two great global powers. Man is caught in a veritable *whirlpool of reduction* where Husserl's 'world of life' is fatally obscured and being is forgotten.[15]

As I write, this political portrait may have become a little dated in the aftermath of the Cold War, but Kundera's point remains, and is chillingly familiar within the memorials of the Christian churches and their celebration of love. For Kundera, the novel, which I expand to the broader reaches of textuality, protects us from the 'forgetting of being' and enables us to celebrate that ambiguity that is life, an infinite complexity in the spirit of continuity, disciplined by the energetic connection of past, present and future in the map of intertextuality. It is this spirit which counters the moral perversity of a world by whose religion 'everything is pardoned in advance and therefore everything cynically permitted'.[16]

If that itself seems cynical, it is only so ironically and stretched against the greater cynicism of a religious rhetoric which pays naive attention to the past and its texts, but actually exercises its authority upon the claims of a future which, because unknown, can engender conformism and pass judgement on almost any terms. To take the rhetoric of a living text seriously in its *ambiguity* is a more difficult and a more costly exercise than the institutions of Western Christianity generally allow. Postmodernity in fiction, it seems to me, is only another way of describing yet a further recognition that the rhetoric of fiction may be endlessly subversive of conventional expectations and almost endlessly stimulating. John Fowles in his fiction *A Maggot* (1985) puts his task as a novelist in religious terms:

> I have long concluded that established religions of any kind are in general the supreme example of forms created to meet no longer existing conditions. If I were asked what the present and future world could best lose or jettison for its own good, I should have no hesitation: all established religion. But its past necessity I do not deny. Least of all do I deny (what novelist could?) that founding stage or moment in all religions, however blind, stale and hidebound they later become, which saw a superseded skeleton must be destroyed, or at least adapted to a new world.[17]

From this most modern, or postmodern, of religious writers of fiction, I would refer you back to my readings of St Mark's Gospel and the epistles of St Paul. There one perceives religious rhetoric in the dangerous and manipulative moment of forming an established religion, for whatever reason. What I have been seeking is a return of language to the founding moment in religion, when always is always now and when there are no vested interests in the preservation of forms or mimetic theories. My rhetorical challenge to religious rhetoric, in so far as it has a form of argument at all, has to be seen both in terms of warp and woof. That is, it is always crossing over itself and making its material out of a suspension of direction. When giving attention to the articulations of the Christian (or, in its different way, the Jewish) tradition, which set such store by history, literature should recognise from within itself the possibility of subverting what is usually taken as a fixed sequence.[18] The fixed sequence of history examines the inheritance of a generation from that which precedes it, the death of the old before the young. But as Derrida has pointed out, the original text is indebted to the translation for its survival. In deconstruction's abolition of the stable subject there is no origination, but either an 'infinite regress of intentionality'[19] or else a recognition that the relationship between Socrates and Plato, or Jesus and Paul is not simply sequential but complex and indeterminate. Jesus survives through Paul, but the claims made by Paul are subverted by the moment of Jesus. Alan Bass, the translator of Derrida's text *The Post Card*, suggests that a reading of the book could be organised around Heidegger's sentence, 'A giving which gives only its gift, but in the giving holds itself back and withdraws, such a giving we call sending.'[20] My concern in this book has been to clear a path for a recovery of a theological sense of gift or grace, which involves a self-reflexive sense of textuality. 'Sending', in Heidegger's use of the term, implies a suspension of the self and a self-objectification (as Paul objectifies himself in his letters to the Christian communities), as well as an unresolved indeterminacy which, in Alan Bass's words, 'leads to questions about destiny – the destiny of "Being" – other than the ones Heidegger asks here'.

This indeterminacy figures most sharply in Derrida's recent work *Of Spirit. Heidegger and the Question* (1987, Trans, 1989) and Derrida's fear of the 'immediate presentation' of thought. On the edge of the abyss, institutions – including the institutions of religion – hold their breath in a wager, an engagement which keeps back and withdraws from the ultimate implications of their language, but offers an affirmation: but to whom is this responsible and what is its status ethically and politically? Both Heidegger and Kant before him, despite their metaphysical suspicion, in different ways, remain complicit with metaphysics in what Derrida describes as 'a nostalgic desire to recover the proper name, the unique name of Being'.[21] In them we have not finally escaped the ambition of the Shemites at Babel – 'shem', after all, means 'name' – a nostalgic ambition which has bedevilled religious rhetoric through the ages.

It is not enough either simply to offer the consolations of mysticism or a negative theology in the tradition of Pseudo-Dionysius, Meister Eckhart or even Georges Bataille, which may be just the comforting back side (as in a post card) of a positive theology, uttering about the seductive scene which it cannot actually see those smug words, 'wish you were here!'

'Irony' in my discussions is to be understood not as a trope of rhetoric (although its origins in this should never be forgotten) but, in Paul de Man's words as 'the systematic undoing . . . of understanding'.[22] Irony, as freedom, is a necessary, though dangerous, freedom within texts, described by Alan Wilde as:

> . . . the typical form, at all levels, of this century's response to the problematics of an increasingly recessive and dissolving self and an increasingly randomized world [which] strives, by constantly reconstituting itself, to achieve the simultaneous acceptance and creation of a world that is both indeterminate and, at the same time, available to consciousness.[23]

I have frequently referred in earlier chapters to Professor Wayne Booth's description of God as supreme ironist, 'infinite but somehow stable'. I simply do not understand Booth's notion of a stable irony except as nostalgia. Certainly the notion of God as the archetypal ironist is neither new nor uncommon. It is present in the Psalms, where God is ironist because he is omniscient, transcendent, infinite and free. As Karl Solger put it early in the nineteenth century:

> Supreme Irony reigns in the conduct of God as he creates men and the life of men. In earthly art Irony has this meaning – conduct similar to God's.[24]

This, of course, begs the question of theology, and it is clear that in the history of literature which presents the infinite deity as an ironist, his characteristics are humour, unpredictability, or, in the case of Thomas Mann in *Lotte in Weimar*, 'at once absolute love and absolute nihilism and indifference'. Heinrich Heine in his *Confessions* of 1854 reflects 'what feeble little jests my most bitter sarcasms were in comparison with His own, and how inferior I was to Him in humour and in giant wit'.[25] And in a letter of 1852 to Louise Colet, Flaubert wrote:

> When will people begin to write down the facts as if it were all a divine joke (*une blague supérieure*), that is to say, as the Lord sees them, from above?[26]

This huge, unstable and destabilising joke which must lie at the very heart of all theology and its texts is precisely what is so threatening to its attempts to establish and maintain a community within a tradition of assent. The power of Christian ideology for centuries shuts out ironic possibilities in its denial of any radical conflict between man and Nature or between man and God.[27] The power which medieval Christendom exercised over its communities became again institutionalised in the authority granted to the texts of scripture in the Reformation, and has continued in the face of the increasing inability of theology to address a contemporary sense of contradiction and dislocation. Only a critical approach to the ambiguity of the texts of our tradition will force us back from the weary retreat into the pseudo-authorities of traditionalism. Yet in our own time, the ghastly trauma of Holocaust has agonisingly silenced the rhetoric of religion, and not only in Christianity. The poetry of Paul Celan has prompted George Steiner to suggest:

> One of the consequences of the Shoah (the Holocaust) is to have transported (violently, irreparably) into

Judaism, both religious and secular, the hermeneutic dilemma . . . in what conceivable language can a Jew speak *to* God after Auschwitz, in what conceivable language can he speak *about* God? The challenge is deeper, more corrosive than that in Christian hermeneutics.[28]

Yet the challenge is to each, and does an ironic response have to be bitter? Pascal, who was certainly conscious enough of the contradictions in the natural world, argued that these contradictions could be resolved only in terms of a supernatural solution. In Steiner's terms, however, this is merely to beg the question, and it is a modern novelist, Alfred de Musil in *The Man Without Qualities* who recognises the confidence trick by which it is claimed that theology, by way of belief in God, guarantees our stability, is actually a trick played upon himself.

By exercising great and manifold skill we manage to produce a dazzling deception by the aid of which we are capable of living alongside the most uncanny things and remaining perfectly calm about it, because we recognise these frozen grimaces of the universe as a table or a chair, a shout or an outstretched arm, a speed or a roast chicken. We are capable of living between one open chasm of the sky above our heads and one slightly camouflaged chasm of the sky beneath our feet, feeling ourselves as untroubled on the earth as in a room with the door locked. We know that life ebbs away both out into the inhuman distances of interstellar space and down into the inhuman construction of the atom-world; but in between there is a stratum of forms that we treat as the things that make up the world, without letting ourselves be in the least disturbed by the fact that this signifies nothing but a preference given to the sense-data received from a certain middle distance. Such an attitude lies considerably below the potentiality of our intellect, but precisely this proves that our feelings play a large part in all this. And in fact the most important intellectual devices produced by mankind serve the preservation of a constant state of mind, and all the emotions, all the passions in the world are a mere nothing compared to the vast but utterly unconscious effort that mankind makes in order to maintain its exalted peace of mind.[29]

Musil's irony seems to me to be immensely liberating, an invitation to abandon the old tricks of religion and embark upon a new theological journey in the spirit of comedy and playful uncertainty, more deeply aware of the pallid seriousness of our constructed terms, and more ready to embrace God's laughter as an infinitely renewable divine comedy. Perhaps, after all, it is an invitation to re-enter the movement towards a new comedy of 'presence',[30] a comedy which recognises Kierkegaard's distinction between rhetorical irony and that true irony which 'does not generally wish to be understood'.[31] Such true irony does not play the rhetorical game of forcing us to choose the ironic location – whether the irony of *Mona Lisa* lies in the ironic smile or in the portrait of someone smiling with silly self-satisfaction. Rather it projects us forward in hope, the hope of Dante's final intuition.

Is it foolishness to end my deconstructive journey on such a note? One might say that irony is inherently tragic in its recognition of the distinction between appearance and reality, and its sense that, in spite of any notion of catharsis, all falls short of expectation, descending into paradox and ambivalence.[32] Over the tragic vision, how-ever, broods in one way or another, from Aeschylus to Thomas Hardy, the grim presence of God. If the modern and postmodern age from Nietzsche has celebrated the death of God, may this perhaps be interpreted as the death of one abiding, coercive tragic vision in the West, the vision of the Grand Inquisitor or of Beckett's lurking, elusive but ever-present Godot? The church, invariably, takes it all too seriously, missing the joke and failing to appreciate the freedom of the risible, laughing, absent, archtetypal ironist God. It prefers the comfortable rhetorical chains of the masters who protect the community from the responsibilities of freedom, the masters, inquisitors and apostles who affirm:

No, to us the weak, too, are dear. They are vicious and rebellious, but in the end they will become obedient too. They will marvel at us and they will regard us as gods because, having become their masters, we consented to endure freedom and rule over them – so dreadful will freedom become to them in the end![33]

I return, then, to the centrality of play and of *enactment*, and to the poetic command to 'do' (ποιῆτε) in our Lord's charge to his disciples. The texts of religion must be played within an endless, provisional game. There is an arbitrariness, indeed, in play, but it is quite different from the arbitrariness of the distinctive rhetoric of religion, at the heart of which lies authoritative proclamation, not rational persuasion (although that is often claimed). We must abandon the second-order discourse of theology, returning to the naughty orators of performance who, like the trickster Salman Rushdie of *The Satanic Verses*, fear no blasphemy but with the supremely ironic cry 'let's get the hell out of here',[34] revel in the freedom and responsibility of language spoken in love and without fear.

Notes

1. W. Shakespeare, *All's Well that Ends Well*. V. 3. 251–2.
2. Stanley Cavell, 'Naughty Orators: Negation of Voice in *Gaslight*', in Sanford Budick and Wolfgang Iser (Eds.), *Languages of the Unsayable. The Play of Negativity in Literature and Literary Theory* (New York, 1989) p. 343.
3. See, Jacques Derrida, *Writing and Difference*. (London, 1978) p. 10, on the distinction between 'text' and 'book'. Also, see Kevin Hart, *The Trespass of the Sign* (Cambridge, 1989) pp. 24–5.

4. Milan Kundera, *The Art of the Novel* p. 7.
5. Ibid. p. 10.
6. Jaroslav Hašek, *The Good Soldier Svejk*. Trans. Cecil Parrott. (Harmondsworth, 1973) p. 139.
7. Derrida, *et al.*, *The Ear of the Other*. Ed. Christie V. McDonald and trans. Peggy Kamuf and Avital Ronell (New York, 1985) p. 102.
8. See, Hart, op. cit. p. 113.
9. J-J, Rousseau, 'A discourse on the origin of inequality', in *The Social Contract and Discourses*. Trans. G.D.H. Cole (London, 1973) p. 99.
10. The phrase, the 'checkmate of rhetoric', is taken from the essay by Kenneth J. Gergen, in Herbert W. Simons (Ed.), *The Rhetorical Turn. Invention and Persuasions in the Conduct of Inquiry* (Chicago, 1990) pp. 293–307.
11. Derrida, *Of Grammatology*, p. 158.
12. See, Kundera, op. cit. pp. 14–20.
13. See, D.C. Muecke, *Irony* (London, 1970) pp. 80–1.
14. Robert Alter, *The Art of Biblical Narrative* (London, 1981).
15. Kundera, op. cit. p. 17.
16. Kundera, *The Unbearable Lightness of Being*. Trans. Michael Henry Heim (London, 1984) p. 4.
17. John Fowles, *A Maggot* (London, 1985) p. 460.
18. For the fullest discussion of this see, J. Derrida, *The Post Card. From Socrates to Freud and Beyond*. Trans. Alan Bass (Chicago, 1987).
19. George Steiner, 'Real Presences' (Cambridge, 1986) p. 13.
20. *The Post Card*. p. xii.
21. Derrida, 'Deconstruction and the other', quoted in Kevin Hart, op. cit. p. 269.
22. Paul de Man, *Allegories of Reading* (New Haven and London, 1979) p. 301.
23. Alan Wilde, *Horizons of Assent* (1971), quoted in D.J. Enright, *The Alluring Problem* p. 4.
24. Quoted in G.G. Sedgewick, *Of Irony, Especially in Drama*. 2nd Ed. (Toronto, 1948) p. 17. See also, generally, D.C. Muecke, op. cit. pp. 37–40, 70–2.
25. *The Poetry and Prose of Heinrich Heine*. Ed. and trans. Frederick Ewen (New York, 1948) p. 489.
26. Quoted in Muecke, op. cit. p. 39.
27. As Muecke puts it, 'it is not surprising that General Irony does not appear in modern Europe until the closed world of Christian ideology loses its power to convince'. op. cit. p. 70.
28. George Steiner, 'The Long Life of Metaphor. An Approach to "the Shoah".' *Encounter*.
29. Alfred de Musil, *The Man Without Qualities*. Trans. Eithne Wilkins and Ernst Kaiser (London, 1961) Vol. II, pp. 275–6.
30. In a letter to me, George Steiner describes his book *Real Presences* (1989) as 'an attempt to "think" the tripartite motion of the *Commedia*'.
31. S. Kierkegaard, *The Concept of Irony*. (London, 1966) p. 266.

32. For an extended discussion of tragedy and catharsis in literature and Christian theology, see Ulrich Simon, *Pity and Terror. Christianity and Tragedy* (London, 1989). A.W. Schlegel was unable to relate the ironic and the tragic. For his contemporary Karl Solger, on the other hand, genuine irony 'begins with the contemplation of the world's fate in the large'. Quoted, René Wellek, *A History of Modern Criticism: The Romantic Age.* (London, 1955) p. 300.

33. F. Dostoyevsky, *The Brothers Karamazov.* 1880. Trans. David Magarshack (Harmondsworth, 1958) Vol. I. p. 297. See also above, Chapter 1 note 28.

34. Salman Rushdie, *The Satanic Verses* (London, 1988) p. 547.

10

A Personal, Inconclusive, Unscientific Postscript: Bearing our Responsibilities

And so where does one go from here, as a responsible theologian? If 'legitimation' was the keyword for Jean-François Lyotard in *The Postmodern Condition* of 1979, then one might suggest that 'responsibility' has become the keyword for our own time, over a decade later. For we have become both more radical, and yet also more conservative as we begin to address the very real ethical, and therefore theological questions thrown up by deconstructionist critical theory.

During the 1980s, the growth of multi-disciplinary research in the field of rhetoric has been a major factor in breaking down barriers which divide disciplines in both scholarship and public affairs. In every sense in the environment of language and argument, theology and religious discourse are linked not only with literary and philosophical discussion, but also with economics, law, political science, social theory and practice. The religious community cannot remain isolated from the questions of power, manipulation and persuasion which lie at the heart of all kinds of community and communicative action.

I am not, any more than Derrida, simply engaged in another project of negative theology, which is generally content simply to remain *detached* from metaphysics, as

150

also from the things of this world.[1] I want to go further than this, distancing myself, like Derrida, from the procedures of such theological endeavour, and defending myself with Derrida's words:

> One would like to consider these procedures a simple rhetoric, even a rhetoric of failure – or worse, a rhetoric that renounces knowledge, conceptual determination, and analysis; for those who have nothing to say or don't want to know anything, it is always easy to mimic the technique of negative theology.[2]

I would want to avoid 'that ontological wager of hyperessentiality'[3] of the negative theology of such as Pseudo-Dionysius and Meister Eckhart, indeed, its inevitability. Where, then, is one allowed (legitimately) to start, let alone finish? Certainly I would remain with Derrida's language, in the language of the unsayable, of 'economy', albeit a paradoxical economy. The importance of this will become, I hope, apparent in a short while.

One begins, in theology, with an evaluation of the pedagogic role. What are we teaching? What are the responsible consequences of our discourse? In this beginning is, if no longer the Word – although it *is* there – then at least the 'subject'. We have, or we should have, lived long enough with our postmodern condition, and if we are to go anywhere from it, as individuals and as an interpretative community, we must do so passionately, and at the same time with a better informed and a wider sense of the tradition than most of us are prepared to possess. Within the community we need to read, think and reflect broadly as well as deeply, with an ever-heightened sense of the close moral connection between *theory* and *praxis*, a sense of rhetorical practice negotiating beyond the artifacts of rhetorical imposition. Lyotard's 1979 *Report* remains pertinent for us. The deconstructive 1980s did not progress much, if at all, with the problem of the collapse of any meta-narrative as a legitimising or unifying force within our experience, and 'theology' on the whole remains oblivious to the radical implications of postmodernity after Nietzsche and Saussure. It could be said, with a supreme cynicism, that our very problems are welcomed as our meta-narrative, but that does not render them any less problematic, any more explanatory. If, in his critical overview, Lyotard emphasises questions of language, or Jürgen Habermas emphasises authority and consensus, then we are bound to address a whole series of questions which theology cannot but consider with the utmost seriousness if it is to retain any possible coherence within our modes of responsible discourse: questions of language and textuality; questions of authority, power and the arts of persuasion which enable them to claim legitimacy; questions of historicism (not least in the re-affirmed cultural materialism of the New Historicist critics); questions of the nature of community; and questions of immanence and transcendence, all need to be revisited and re-examined.

As literary critics, theologians or students of rhetoric, our business is increasingly, and more overtly, political, and its aesthetics have changed, becoming more elusive and more difficult. In hope, after Ernst Bloch, after Bakhtin, in a 'post-Marxist' and 'post-Christian' era, we must commit ourselves to dialogue, textuality, discussion and endless, open discourse. But, equally, we need to be aware of the nature of such commitment, for it is not to the positing of any necessary textual identity claim. As appears to be the case of Habermas in *The Philosophical Discourse of Modernity* (1985), on the other hand, it is not afraid that postmodern indeterminacy will confound political discourse or moral – even theological – possibilities.[4] Insofar as Habermas' programme is centrally situated within the tradition of Western metaphysics, cementing discourse with discourse, one must be bold to take one's leave of it, and on moral grounds. Why so?

It may be, at this stage, that we can no longer afford to desire meaning, conclusion, definition. That is, one should be prepared to abandon the deceits of such desire. That, in itself, is a simple and even naive statement, but it may partake of a Ricoeurean second naïveté, depending on where it is situated. If one wants to *relate* responsibly to that terrible primal scene of persuasion in Paradise, which underwrites all our need for theology, it must be a relationship of endless, unendurable differing and deferral, its acceptance never in the present tense, yet nevertheless intensely present.

I have asked myself, who have been the significant writers and thinkers with whom I have most closely lived during the writing of this book. I do not mean the great literary figures who are always with us – Euripides, Shakespeare, some biblical and liturgical texts: nor *the* important thinkers, those you cannot escape from in our tradition, like Kant, Nietzsche and Heidegger. I have to say, Georges Bataille and Jean Baudrillard. Why these? It is because these writers address most acutely in their textuality and their economy the problems of nihilism, power and violence, which interest me not so much because they are an inescapable part of our socio-political experience in the twentieth century, but because they lurk so insistently in the primal scenes embedded in the language, syntax and rhetoric of that comfortable, reassuring theological tradition which we so often inherit through the churches and their liturgies, ethics, and aesthetics. You begin to feel the force of this violence when you move out onto the boundaries and edges of sacred texts and institutions, for example, into the strong feminist readings in the Book of Judges of Mieke Bal, reversing established priorities. The nature of power and persuasiveness is revealed when 'what is seen to be central [is] marginalised, and what has been treated as marginal [is] become central'.[5]

If thought is not to be a mere simulacrum, it must remain conscious both of its relativity and the price of freedom. A self-consciousness that does not flinch or turn away from itself, as Bataille expressed it, will always live on the boundary, escaping that cohesion to live within which is death, and risking that violence whose ultimate, unacceptable turmoil may allow the recasting of the sacred.[6] Violence increasingly concerns me as I feel myself to be its victim, not least from within the texts of that which claims to offer comfort and salvation. And not only I, but all of us who shelter within a religious 'tradition'.

Following Baudrillard's theory of industrial society through his early Marxist *critique* of capitalism, to the abandonment of the productivist metaphor in Marxism, to a world of simulacra beyond representation, may be a journey along a rhetorical highway to pessimism and nihilism. Yet within such post-structuralism, as within Bataille's 'general economy' of a theory of religion, wherein violence is no longer deployed self-destructively inwardly, but is turned to the outside, questions of value are represented. In this sense, value is neither an inherent property of things, nor an arbitrary projection of subjects (as in so much rhetoric) but rather 'the product of the dynamics of some economy or, indeed, of any number of economies . . . in relation to the shifting state of which an object or entity will have a different (shifting) value'.[7] It may be that the apparently deeply pessimistic hyperlogic of Baudrillardian consumerism harbours a response, in its very extremity, in a double negation, to the Egalitarian Fallacy, which is the notion that a denial of objective or essential value entails a commitment to the view that all judgements are 'equally valid' or 'good'.[8] Actually, just as negative theology in Derrida's sense, feeds off the assumptions of other theologies, so this Fallacy merely feeds off the conviction of the validity of its opposite – that an essentialist view of values is the only measure of the value of utterances.

If, however, value judgements are themselves perceived as commodities within an economy, even – or especially – a collapsing economy, they may become indicators towards the realisation that, within conditions of interest and ambition there is no such thing as an honest opinion, since no judgement is unaffected by the power demands of its particular social and institutional conditions. The whole argument may easily be regarded in the context of my discussion of the community of St Mark's Gospel, in Chapter 4. Finally, at the extreme collapse of all 'economic' interests, in the ultimate achievement of Baudrillard's hyperlogic,[9] questions of value may actually be purified in the face of the unacceptable limit, before that which can only be rejected in an unutterable, awful moment, and a deconstructive, divine moment of revulsion beyond fear. The only conditions for value judgements are then *conditions of possibility*, without prejudice or interest.

The point may be illustrated by a reflection upon the recent film of the notorious *Last Exit to Brooklyn*. After reading the book, one recognises that a problem with the film is that the violence there cinematically depicted is simply not violent enough. The savage street gang muggings and, above all, the repeated rape of the prostitute Tralala *should* be unbearable for those watching. Only then can their violence be exorcised of the voyeurism and morbidity which pervade the film, of which the aesthetic rhetoric turns violently in upon itself without cathartic possibility. Like the implicit violence of so much religious rhetoric, not least in the liturgy, the explicit violence of the film contributes to a nasty mixture of just-about permissible excitement, vague human sympathy for suffering humanity, and the voyeuristic sense that *we*, anyway, can stand apart from such brutish behaviour.

One must learn to abandon that kind of nostalgia for lost presences which Derrida, ultimately, perceives in Heidegger. One cannot afford to repress the anxiety engendered by such powerful inherited influences which falsely claim to protect our moral identity, and turn always back upon the pretence at argument. There is always that easy way out, the way of Harold Bloom in the ruin of sacred truths,[10] in a revived romanticism which cloaks a sinister gnosticism. The old heresies are always the most dangerous, for obvious reasons. For they have survived the longest, their rhetoric well tested.

What then of the violence which is unendurable? René Girard discussed the matter deftly, but his *Violence and the Sacred* (1972) is an extremely violent text, another example, I suggest, of academic rhetoric, too clever and carefully essentialist. Are we prepared, at this stage, in Girard's words 'to expose to the light of reason the role played by violence in human society'?[11] Any sense that we might *understand* or encompass violence, as Girard implies, or 'fashion something' from its wreckage, as Ernest Becker wanted to propose in *The Denial of Death* (1973), moves far too quickly through the traumas of postmodernity with undue sweet reasonableness and enlightenment optimism. Theologically, I suggest, and in fear of religious rhetoric, there is a primary need to face rhetorically the unacceptable, unbearable face of violence. For the alternatives are the almost inevitable voyeurism of the film of *Last Exit to Brooklyn*, or the implicit violence done to the reader by the structured discourses of Girard and Becker. But how can art or theology 'embody', incarnate, the unacceptable and the unbearable? This extreme, ultimate contradiction in terms entails a radical deconstruction which risks encountering the profound unknowability of the divine (perhaps) not merely by detachment – the general tendency of negative theology – but by relinquishing any clinging to the metaphysical illusion or rational possibility. Any choice must be pure, radical, ultimate.

Girard himself acknowledges that 'metaphysical desire always ends in enslavement, failure and shame'.[12] If left unchecked the hierarchal impulse which is all too evident in the Western religious tradition, in spite of its celebratory, carnival claims, results in a mastery which becomes blasé, and therefore potentially masochistic. We return again to the model of Dostoyevsky's Grand Inquisitor. Girard describes the religious impulse behind Dostoyevsky's parable shrewdly:

By a misunderstanding even more remarkable than those which preceded it, he [the masochist] now chooses to see in shame, defeat, and enslavement not the inevitable results of an aimless faith and an absurd mode of behaviour but rather the *signs* of divinity and the preliminary condition of all metaphysical success. Henceforth the subject bases his enterprise of autonomy on failure; he founds his *project* of being God on an abyss.[13]

Such language may be seen as a chilling indictment of a religious tradition which too often has revelled in human failure and inadequacy and of which the authoritarian structures rhetorically encourage enslavement by the promise of salvation. The masochistic consequences are acutely apparent in the modern instance of the brilliant and tragic Simone Weil. The consequences for metaphysics are described by Derrida in the quotation from Anatole France which I have already noted,[14] wherein is done away all the particularities of the responsible individual, the specifics of value.

The human degradation implied by such *theological* strategies for universal claims is starkly and crudely exposed by Dennis Potter in his novel *Blackeyes* (1987), which in its early pages bleakly portrays the selection procedures for a model to market a brand of body lotion. As the carefully selected girls anonymously prepare for the audition, the male organiser explains the purpose of the procedures.

'The basic idea here,' he said, concentrating on the interruption, 'is that of a timeless space in a timeless nowhere and everywhere. – '
A sigh warned him to come back from the woods where a French semiologist lay mouldering, in piles of fallen leaves that had long since given up their signals. Stilk knew that he was employed to rattle the stick

in the swill-bucket, but his self-hatred was not eased
by the sure fact that nobody in his audience ever had
the slightest idea of the provenance of this particular
reference.[15]

The basic idea is the achievement of the ambition of those
'metaphysicians' who would grind away the particular-
ity of all coinage, all the specific qualities which make it
immediate, valuable, individual and necessary, and replace it with the faceless, timeless quality which claims
'inestimable value' in infinite space. In such suspension,
rhetoric then may *claim* a bottom line, persuading us to
buy and be persuaded – but at what human cost? In
Potter's narrative, the crudity is extreme and deliberate:

> 'Let's get to the bottom line. Let's chew on the nitty-
> gritty. What we want here is a blonde with terrific tits
> who's got the sense to make love to the fucking bot-
> tle.'[16]

The profound sense of alienation and embarrassment
arises out of the public exposure of human degradation.
In advertising, in the public art of theological persuasion,
it happens so often that we can barely remember to dis-
approve. On the whole the public practice of art and
theology has learnt the rhetorical necessity of being
acceptable, or using morality as a cloak for deception.
The use of a post mortem heaven and hell as levers to
make children, or communities, behave properly, is a
familiar enough strategy. We work and worship within
structures and institutions of one kind or another, and
need to survive within them. Yet I sense that, in the end,
that is the tragedy of theology and also the possibility of
a theology. For it implies a scandal, and the painful
realisation has to dawn that the scandal can never be
enough, and perhaps, in the first instance like irony, can
only be honest in intense privacy.

Irony, I have already suggested, is both unstable and private, buried deep within the manipulations of public textuality.[17] So Georges Bataille 'renders him[self] similar to God, similar to nothing' (that approximation is crucial), while Blanchot in *Thomas the Obscure* writes towards nothing, out of textuality. Then something has to begin again beyond the lost currency of the onto-epistemological tradition which has sustained, and has been sustained by, our theological languages. Values need to be reformulated, responsibilities reassumed – lived.

Still nobody has got much further than Nietzsche, or actually persuaded us (in the rhetorical sense) that there is any viable alternative to his final insanity, given the blatant insanity of our own century of violence and pitiful theological and philosophical excuses. Derrida accuses Heidegger of 'a nostalgic desire to recover the proper name'. Habermas, it has been suggested,[18] presents himself as having appropriated the tragedy of Heidegger, which Heidegger himself could never wholly admit. Either way, adding layers of discourse over the yawning abyss of postmodernity, presenting a rhetorical justification, is neither ethical nor safe. Do we then need a new harrowing of this hellish abyss?

In the light of all that I have said, where can one begin to represent any theological possibility, assuming that one still wants to do so? The question actually leads me back to an earlier question, that is, how does art or theology *embody* the unacceptable and the unbearable, scripturally, the 'glory' (δόζα) of God? In my concluding pages, I wish to deal in some detail with one great pre-Christian tragedy, Euripides' *The Bacchae* (406 B.C.), in a final exercise in intra-textuality, proposing the play as a startling mirror image of Christ's Passion.

The Bacchae has been described as celebrating 'the death of the god, the lament for vanished life, and the resurrection amid songs of jubilation'.[19] It seems to me to be far more problematic and dialectical than that, an incursion,

160   *Rhetoric, Power and Community*

into madness, violent possession and ritual dismemberment (σπαραγμός).[20] The boy–king Pentheus, is by his very name in Greek, a 'man of sorrow', initially adolescent, at odds with himself and divinity – as Dionysus expresses it in his opening speech 'a fighter against God'. Pentheus' condition is an invitation for the god to show his power. His eventual death by bloody dismemberment at the hands of his mother Agave and her fellow Bacchic revellers, is a wild celebration with strong suggestions of incest and cannibalism. To the Christian tradition – particularly in the light of ancient criticisms of the eucharistic sacrifice – the process of the play is full of uncomfortable overtones. Even in his own time, was Euripides offering a grim satire upon religion, a mirror image?

In this instance, I am inclined to agree with Girard that the power or 'meaning' of *The Bacchae* arises out of its 'fertile incoherence', its lack of equilibrium, its refusal to admit 'the Manichaean division between good and evil'.[21] Dionysus' 'medicine' (φάρμακον) is both a 'poison' and a 'cure', the god himself an unnerving, vaguely androgynous, combination of energy and control. But, as has often been critically noted,[22] one aspect of Dionysus is omitted by Euripides – his role as the victim of sacrifice, the dying god. In *The Bacchae*, that part is taken by Pentheus, who here becomes the scapegoat (φαρμακός) suffering ritual dismemberment. To the Christian mind, nurtured on scriptural imagery and the Fourth Gospel, Agave's fearful chant as she shows Pentheus' severed head to the now-terrified chorus, sounds a heavy irony in its choice of imagery:

> I am bringing home from the mountains
> A vine-branch freshly cut,
> For the gods have blessed our hunting.[23]

Pentheus, certainly, is a grotesque, human imitation of Christ. Truly a victim, without redemption, his dismemberment lies at the heart of a play which warns against the daemonic invasion resulting from both repression and inquiring too far – Pentheus' voyeuristic intrusion upon the liberated, celebratory revellers. As R.D. Stock has expressed it, 'in his distinctive way, Euripides may be expressing the Socratic ideal of knowing we know nothing, *docta ignorantia*'.[24]

Who can ever know what it is to know nothing? Bataille's question returns insistently. *The Bacchae* is a crucial text, its themes of seduction, power, celebration, chaos, carnival and fragmentation haunting our post-modern literature. In a world where we already *live* the unthinkable, perhaps the only way to endure and survive is to begin to learn to *think* the unthinkable,[25] following Socrates into that new Platonism, with all its rhetorical suspicion, to which I alluded in my opening pages. Arguing against Aristotelian defences of rhetoric brings about a recognition that language, of course, is powerful, a 'great prince' able to transform human experience,[26] able, it may be to transform the dark irony of Agave's speech into the irony of liberation and freedom, the irony of God's creative laughter.

But that means bearing to think the unthinkable: embodying in textuality the unbearable so that the embodiment and incarnation endures and embraces its own fragmentation and dismemberment. The text itself then becomes the sacred space of eucharistic celebration, not a mimetic image, but the place of enactment and memorial. Being many, it is one, the text being that from, by and through which one 'gets "the hell" out' in both senses.

All that a poet (as Wilfrid Owen knew), a theologian or a teacher can do is show a dismembered, embodying text, purged of the demons of continuity. Dismemberment must become a part of our very textuality (upon whose integrity we pride ourselves), a fragmentation within an exposed, defenceless discourse which merely offers itself and its drama, gratuitously, for fear and pity, to effect the proper catharsis which may allow the possibility of theological renewal.

The Christian image of the crucified Christ now replaces the shredded figure of Pentheus, Dionysus himself reassuming his true role as sacrificial victim. The blasphemy is so extreme that interpretation is suspended and is only possible again through a radical renewal – a resurrection of body and embodying text. The risk of the business, of course, is extreme, ultimately beyond moral and aesthetic categories, but must be tested every inch of the way and by every instrument at our critical disposal. Only then can the breakage and forsakenness of Mark 15: 34 be sufficiently radical, the irony complete and the power of rhetoric exposed.

In what sense do the haunting, unexpurgated images of the Christian tradition and the bloody dismemberment of the eucharistic sacrifice lie behind the preoccupations of this book, images, I have suggested, awaiting continual release from the shoddy, protective structures of system and social institution? Dealing with the traditions of rhetoric, and taking the radical textuality of the postmodern condition seriously is a nasty business, long overdue for most, if not all of us. But theologically, I believe, it is unavoidable.

Notes

1. See, Kevin Hart, *The Trespass of the Sign* (Cambridge, 1989) p. 267.
2. Jacques Derrida, 'How to avoid speaking: denials'. Trans. Ken Frieden, in Sanford Budick and Wolfgang Iser (eds), *Languages of the Unsayable*. (New York, 1989) pp. 4–5.
3. Ibid. p. 8.
4. See, George A. Trey, 'The Philosophical Discourse of Modernity: Habermas's Postmodern Adventure'. *Diacritics*. 19.2 (1989) 78–9.
5. Mieke Bal, *Death and Dissymmetry* (Chicago and London, 1988) p. 2.
6. See, Georges Bataille, *Theory of Religion*. Trans. Robert Hurley. (New York, 1989) esp. p. 10.
7. Barbara Herrnstein Smith, 'Value Without Truth-Value', in John

Fekete (ed.), *Life After Postmodernism. Essays on Value and Culture.* (London, 1988) pp. 1–2.
8. See, ibid. p. 8.
9. See above, pp. 112–13.
10. See, Harold Bloom, *Ruin the Sacred Truths. Poetry and Belief from the Bible to the Present.* (Cambridge, Mass., 1989).
11. René Girard, *Violence and the Sacred.* Trans. Patrick Gregory. (Baltimore and London, 1977; first publ. 1972) p. 318.
12. Girard, *Deceit, Desire and the Novel.* Trans. Yvonne Freccero (Baltimore and London, 1965) p. 176.
13. Ibid. p. 177.
14. See above, p. 124.
15. Dennis Potter, *Blackeyes* (London, 1987) p. 22.
16. Ibid. p. 23.
17. See above, p. 133.
18. By David E. Klemm, in an unpublished paper entitled 'Two Ways to Avoid Tragedy'.
19. Gerardus van der Leeuw, *Sacred and Profane Beauty: The Holy in Art.* Trans. David E. Green (New York, 1963) p. 91.
20. Much of what follows in my discussion was inspired by conversations with Robert Detweiler of Emory University, Atlanta.
21. Girard, *Violence and the Sacred*, pp. 126–42.
22. See, for example, R.D. Stock, *The Flutes of Dionysus. Daemonic Enthrallment in Literature* (Nebraska, 1989) p. 8.
23. Euripides, *The Bacchae.* Trans. Philip Vellacott (Penguin Classics, Harmondsworth, 1970), p. 218.
24. Stock, op. cit. p. 10.
25. See, Robert Detweiler, 'Apocalyptic Fiction and the End(s) of Realism', in David Jasper and Colin Crowder. Eds., *European Literature and Theology in the Twentieth Century: Ends of Time* (London, 1990) pp. 181–2.
26. See, Jane P. Tompkins, Introduction to *Reader-Response Criticism: From Formalism to Post-Structuralism* (Baltimore and London, 1980) p. xxv.

Select Bibliography

This bibliography is not exhaustive, and is intended merely as an introductory guide to the enormous, and growing, literature on rhetoric. Its purpose is to enable the reader to pursue some of the themes of the present study, and also to indicate certain works which have particularly influenced me in the writing of it.

I   RHETORIC

Wayne C. Booth, *The Rhetoric of Fiction* (Chicago, London, 1969).

Wayne C. Booth, *Modern Dogma and the Rhetoric of Assent* (Chicago, 1974).

Kenneth Burke, *The Rhetoric of Religion. Studies in Logology* (Berkeley, 1970).

Paul de Man, *Allegories of Reading* (Yale, 1979).

Peter Dixon, *Rhetoric* (London, 1971).

Stanley Fish, 'Withholding the Missing Portion: power, meaning and persuasion in Freud's *The Wolf Man*', in Fabb, Attridge, Durant and MacCabe (Eds.), *The Linguistics of Writing* (Manchester, 1987).

Stanley Fish, *Doing What Comes Naturally. Change, Rhetoric, and the Practice of Theory in Literary and Legal Studies* (Durham, N.C., 1989).

George A. Kennedy, *Classical Rhetoric and its Christian and Secular Tradition from Ancient to Modern Times* (Chapel Hill, 1980).

George A. Kennedy, *New Testament Interpretation through Rhetorical Criticism* (Chapel Hill, 1984).

James L. Kinneavy, *Greek Rhetorical Origins of Christian Faith* (Oxford, 1987).

David E. Klemm, 'Toward a Rhetoric of Postmodern

Theology: Through Barth and Heidegger.' *Journal of the American Academy of Religion*, LV (1987) 443-69.

David E. Klemm, 'Ricoeur, Theology and the Rhetoric of Overturning'. *Literature and Theology III* (1989) 267–84.

Heinrich Lausberg, *Handbuch der Literarischen Rhetorik.* 2 vols. (Munich, 1960).

Walter Nash, *Rhetoric: The Wit of Persuasion* (Oxford, 1989).

Nelson, Megill and McCloskey (Eds.), *The Rhetoric of the Human Sciences* (Wisconsin, 1987).

Chaim Perelman and L. Olbrechts-Tyteca, *The New Rhetoric: A Treatise on Argumentation* (Notre Dame, 1971).

Chaim Perelman, *The New Rhetoric and the Humanities* (Dordrecht, 1979).

Chaim Perelman, *The Realm of Rhetoric.* Trans. William Kluback (Notre Dame, 1982).

Plato, *Phaedrus.* Trans, Walter Hamilton (Harmondsworth, 1973).

Debora K. Shuger, *Sacred Rhetoric. The Christian Grand Style in the English Renaissance* (Princeton, 1988).

Herbert W. Simons (Ed.) *The Rhetorical Turn. Invention and Persuasion in the Conduct of Inquiry* (Chicago, 1990).

Stephen Tyler, *The Unspeakable: Discourse, Dialogue and Rhetoric in the Postmodern World* (Wisconsin, 1987).

Richard Whateley, *Elements of Rhetoric* 4th Edn. (Oxford, 1832).

Amos Wilder, *Early Christian Rhetoric* (Harvard, 1971).

Wilhelm Wuellner, 'Paul's Rhetoric of Argumentation in Romans.' *Catholic Biblical Quarterly* 38 (1976) 330–51.

Wilhelm Wuellner, *Hermeneutics and Rhetorics. Scriptura.* Special Issue. (Stellenbosch, 1989).

II IRONY

Wayne C. Booth, *A Rhetoric of Irony* (Chicago, London, 1974).

D.J. Enright, *The Alluring Problem. An Essay on Irony* (Oxford, 1988).

Søren Kierkegaard, *The Concept of Irony: with constant reference to Socrates*, 1841. Trans. Lee M. Capel (London, 1966).

D.C. Muecke, *Irony* (London, 1970).

Richard Rorty, *Contingency, Irony, and Solidarity* (Cambridge, 1989).

Jonathan Swift, *A Modest Proposal* (1729).

III   GENERAL

Mikhail Bakhtin, *Rabelais and His World*. Trans. Helene Iswolsky (Bloomington, 1984).

Georges Bataille, *My Mother, Madame Edwarda, The Dead Man* Trans. Austryn Wainhouse (London, New York, 1989).

Jean Baudrillard, *Selected Writings* (Oxford, 1988).

Sanford Budick and Wolfgang Iser (Eds.), *Languages of the Unsayable. The Play of Negativity in Literature and Literary Theory* (New York, 1989).

Joseph A. Buttigeig (Ed.), *Criticism without Boundaries. Directions and Crosscurrents in Postmodern Critical Theory* (Notre Dame, 1987).

Jacques Derrida, 'The White Mythology: Metaphor in the Text of Philosophy'. *New Literary History* 6 (1974) 5–74.

Jacques Derrida, *Of Grammatology*. Trans. Gayatri Chakravorty Spivak (Baltimore, 1976; first publ. 1967).

Jacques Derrida, *Writing and Difference* Trans. Alan Bass (Chicago, 1978).

Euripides, *The Bacchae and Other Plays*. Trans. Philip Vellacott (Harmondsworth, 1970).

Arthur Evans, *The God of Ecstasy. Sex Roles and the Madness of Dionysos* (New York, 1988).

Stanley Fish, *Self-Consuming Artifacts. The Experience of Seventeenth Century Literature* (Los Angeles, London, 1972).

Stanley Fish, *Is There a Text in This Class? The Authority of Interpretive Communities* (Harvard, 1980).

René Girard, *Violence and the Sacred*. Trans. Patrick Gregory (Baltimore, London, 1977; first publ. 1972).

Jürgen Habermas, *The Philosophical Discourse of Modernity* Trans. Frederick Lawrence (Cambridge, 1987; first publ. 1985).

Kevin Hart, *The Trespass of the Sign. Deconstruction, Theology and Philosophy* (Cambridge, 1989).

David Jasper and R.C.D. Jasper (Eds.), *Language and the Worship of the Church* (London, 1990).

Milan Kundera, *The Art of the Novel*. Trans. Linda Asher (London, 1988).

C.S. Lewis, *Poetry and Prose in the Sixteenth Century* (Oxford, 1954).

Friedrich Nietzsche, *Twilight of the Idols* 1889. Trans. R.J. Hollingdale (Harmondsworth, 1990).

Friedrich Nietzsche, *The Anti-Christ* 1895. Trans. R.J. Hollingdale (Harmondsworth, 1990).

Elaine Pagels, *Adam, Eve and the Serpent* (London, 1988).

Richard Rorty, *Consequences of Pragmatism* (Minneapolis, 1972).

Richard Rorty, *Philosophy and the Mirror of Nature* (Oxford, 1989).

Robert P. Scharlemann, *Inscriptions and Reflections. Essays in Philosophical Theology* (Charlottesville, 1989).

Robert Scholes, *Textual Power. Literary Theory and the Teaching of English* (Yale, 1985).

Graham Shaw, *The Cost of Authority* (London, 1983).

George Steiner, *Real Presences* (London, 1989).

R.D. Stock, *The Flutes of Dionysus. Daemonic Enthrallment in Literature*, (Nebraska, 1989).

Gianni Vattimo, *The End of Modernity. Nihilism and Hermeneutics in Post-Modern Culture*. Trans. Jon R. Snyder (Oxford, 1988).

James Boyd White, *When Words Lose Their Meaning. Constitutions and Reconstitutions of Language, Characters and Community* (Chicago, London, 1984).

Walter Wink, *Naming the Powers* (Philadelphia, 1984).

Index